FIGHTING FOR APARTHEID : A JOB FOR LIFE

European Citizens in the South African Defence Force

Preface by Dr. C.F. Beyers Naudé

968

Fighting for Apartheid: A Job for Life was first
published by the Anti Apartheid Movement
Netherlands (AABN) in september 1988

Alman Metten is Member of European
Parliament for the Dutch Labour Party,
dr. Paul Goodison is his research-assistant.

Please order your copies from:
AABN, P.O. Box 10.500, 1001 EM Amsterdam,
Netherlands, tel. (0)20-267525
COSAWR, B.M. Box 2190, London WC1N 3XX
England, tel. 1-2786928

For information on the Apartheid war and
the South African war resistance also
contact COSAWR Netherlands, P.O. Box 543,
1000 AN Amsterdam, tel. (0)20 - 185802.

£3.00
ISBN 90-70367-10-6

TABLE OF CONTENTS

Preface

Apartheid society is increasingly falling under the spell of violence.
There is a far-reaching process of militarization: the army takes action
in the townships, is often even present in the schools, is present in
Namibia and raids the frontline countries. This violence makes our
society sick and claims numerous casualties.
The armed forces need more men to keep the situation "under control".
Virtually all men, young or less young, are now deployed to maintain a
hopeless situation.
Since a few years holders of foreign passports who live in South Africa
are also conscripted into the South African Defence Force. By now
the acts of war have reached the doorstep of every white house.
Every white family has become familiar with the war because either one
of their sons is in the armed forces, or a cousin, or the boy next door.
Geographically remote as the war may seem to whites, it has come
very near at the same time. When questioned later on about his physical
involvement, nobody will be able to say: "I didn't know about it".
It is gratifying that a large number of young whites has been courageous
enough to resist the war. They are those who do not report for their call up,
who go into hiding or leave the country. They are the brave boys who
come out for peace publicly; young men like David Bruce, like the 143
who refuse to take service. They follow their consciences. They refuse
to point the barrels of their rifles at their protesting countrymen whom
they do not consider their enemies. They are looking for a way out of
racialism. They have made clear that they feel responsible for the
future of the country. Imprisonment awaits them; the End Conscription
Campaign is banned by now.
Their stand requires international solidarity and active support from
Europe. Because as this book points out, one third of South Africa's
whites consists of European nationals or people entitled to a European
nationality. This publication shows the far-reaching consequences of
conscription in South Africa and the hitherto unknown part played by
holders of European passports. It makes clear that the violence in
South Africa has equally become the responsibility of the governments
in the countries of the European Community. Therefore I hope that
Europe will support the brave men in South Africa and will take its own
measures to prevent European subjects from fighting for Apartheid.

Dr. C.F. Beyers Naudé

INTRODUCTION

Condemnation of Apartheid is in the civilised world almost an article of faith, adhered to by people of all political convictions. By now, however, we have passed the stage of condemnation in word only. For the sake of dismantling Apartheid, almost all countries in the world are applying economic sanctions against South Africa. The European Community, however, the world's largest commercial unit and South Africa's major trading partner and investor, is clearly lagging behind in the area of sanctions. In itself this is already an embarrassing situation for the Community, but this brochure will point out that the connections between the European Community and South Africa are much closer even than that.

Over one third of white South Africans are nationals of an EC country. In 1984 over 82% of this group are South African nationals at the same time. The remaining eighteen percent were nationals of an EC country only. Many of these European South Africans have fled to South Africa from Rhodesia, Mozambique and Angola. Nevertheless, because of their EC passports or their right to acquire one, they can easily return to the Community should things become too hot for them in South Africa. Such a mass return would mainly be a threat to countries like the United Kingdom and Portugal, but the other EC countries cannot afford to disregard this possibility. The implementation of the internal market will mean that these South Africans can settle down anywhere in the Community. The possibility that they will settle down in the European Community makes it even more relevant to know what is the part played by them at present in bolstering Apartheid.

This brochure will make clear that the South African government, because of its increasing need for sufficient manpower to curb black resistance at home and at the same time to keep Namibia occupied and to destabilise the neighbouring countries, has gradually incorporated the white holders of European passports into the South African armed forces. To the white male inhabitants, living and working in South Africa means lifelong military involvement in bolstering Apartheid. Between the age of 20 and 32 (after two years full-time conscription) they have to spend 16.6% of their working hours in the armed forces, after 32 years of age, a further 6.7%.

Because of this presence of European South Africans in the South African armed forces, by now over one third of these forces consist of whites who possess or are entitled to an EC passport. The actions by the South African Defence Force in black areas, the illegal occupation of Namibia, the destabilising actions in the frontline countries and the permanent occupation of southern Angola have been condemned time and again by the EC governments, but a considerable part of all this is carried out by EC subjects!

This paradoxical situation is at the least remarkable, but perhaps even more remarkable is that when these facts were revealed (e.g. in the European Parliament in February 1986[1]) this did not prompt any action by member countries. The member countries prefer to disregard their responsibility. Thus the measures approved under considerable public pressure by the EC on 10 September 1985, specifically the "refusal to cooperate in the military sphere" with South Africa are meaningless, since it is hard to see how the mass participation of EC subjects in the South African armed forces could fail to fall under this heading. All this is even stranger as South Africa's destabilisation campaigns threaten and destroy development projects financed by both the Community and individual member states. Limited non-lethal military aid is now at last being rendered for the protection of these projects but those EC citizens who, as South African conscripts or professional soldiers, are responsible for this destabilisation, remain just as welcome in the Community, where they may reside with impunity.

The situation is yet more absurd. Several EC countries along with South Africa are co-signatories of a treaty which exempts dual nationals from military service if service has already been rendered in one of the countries to which the citizen owes allegiance. This means that the fulfilment of military service obligations in South Africa, or even Namibia, provides an exemption from military service in some European countries. These facts place the Community's condemnation of Apartheid and its poor package of sanctions in a very different light. If this is not malicious negligence, it is at least serious complicity.

This complicity applies to European companies as well. This does not refer to the compulsory payment of taxes, but rather to the voluntary supplementary payments that conscripts receive up to the level of their civil salaries. As South African men spend a considerable part of their economically active lives in the armed forces, significant amounts are involved. The voluntary supplementary payments by industry make sure that the South African armed forces keep contented recruits at their disposal. All this is not really "neutral" towards Apartheid. Nor does it provide the ideal case for argueing against disinvestment.

In this brochure we will investigate to what extent South African society has become militarised; the interests and involvement of European citizens and companies in the armed defence of Apartheid and in the war in the whole of Southern Africa; the reactions of European governments to this situation and the response from within South Africa itself.

(1) Official Journal, Debates of the European Parliament, no. 2-335 February, 1986, p. 257.

2 THE MILITARISATION OF SOUTH AFRICAN SOCIETY

.1 Introduction

European citizens have been involved in the various components of the SADF for many years, be it as professional full-time soldiers, full-time or part-time conscripts or part-time commando volunteers. The various components of the SADF have been allocated specific, yet flexibly defined tasks which together form part of an integrated defence strategy. Prior to the extension of conscription in 1982 and 1984 few European citizens who were not also South African citizens showed any marked enthusiasm for serving in the SADF and voluntary participation rates were extremely low. Similarly, South African citizens who were not obliged to undertake military service showed a marked lack of enthusiasm for "weekend soldiering". This situation began to take on serious dimensions for the government, as resistance to the oppression of Apartheid mounted. As manpower constraints became increasingly apparent, so the South African government began to increase the level of compulsion to render military service. This applied in particular to two of the mainstay elements of the SADF, the Citizen Force and the Commando. It is to the various structures of the SADF that we now turn.

.2 Structure of the South African Defence Force (SADF)

a) a full-time **Permanent Force** of professional soldiers,
b) a **Citizen Force** including those undergoing two year periods of full-time national service and part-time conscripts,
c) a **Commando** system of localised militia groups initially consisting of part-time volunteers but since 1982 increasingly relying on conscription of older adult males.

In each of these elements of the SADF men with citizenship of a European Community member state and men eligible for citizenship of a Community Member State have been, and are increasingly, actively participating in the defence of Apartheid.

COMPOSITION OF THE SOUTH AFRICAN ARMY AFTER 1982

Permanent Force (PF)   Regular full-time professional soldiers (volunteers).

Citizen Force (CF)	Conscripts undergoing their initial two years training and service (18-20 years of age), and a part-time force subject to conscription commitments (20-32 years of age). Legally this includes those doing their national service, but it popularly refers only to those doing periods of duty after they have completed their initial national service.
Commandos	Locally based militia's responsible for the defence of the area in which they are based. Until 1982 a largely volunteer force but since 1982 increasingly based on conscription (32-55 years of age).
Controlled National Reserve	All ex-SADF members and conscripts who have finished all previous service commitments will be transfered to this reserve until they are 65. To be called up in an emergency.

In 1983 during an exchange in the British House of Commons it was revealed that at least 300 former British soldiers were serving as professional soldiers in the Permanent Force of the SADF, including at least 50 Officers (this represented 2.5% of whites in the Permanent Force) many of whom retained their rank in the British Reserve Force.[2] In addition to these British soldiers (many of whom moved south after the independence of Zimbabwe) a substantial number of former Portuguese army personnel came over to the Permanent Force, following the collapse of Portuguese colonial rule in Mozambique and Angola. These former Portuguese military personnel have played an important role in South Africa's aggressive campaign of regional destabilisation.

Even prior to the extension of conscription to the white immigrant community in South Africa in April 1984, figures from 1976 indicate that on average some 1,765 non-South African citizens were undergoing voluntary national service at any one time[3]; with a number of them dying in defence of Apartheid often hundreds of miles beyond South Africa's borders in northern Namibia and southern Angola. Within the immigrant community however, only a small proportion (some 6%) of the under 30s were volunteering to fight in defence of Apartheid.[4]

2.3 Commandos for Area Defence
In many respects the attitude of the immigrant community was symptomatic of the attitude of that component of South African

(2) Sunday Tribune, 10.4.83. (3) Rand Daily Mail, 15.9.83.
(4) 1,765 out of 28,939 aged under 30, Rand Daily Mail, 15.9.83.

citizenry who until 1982 were not eligible for compulsory military service but who, on a voluntary basis, were expected to render service to what became increasingly the cornerstone of the military defence strategy, the Commandos. Prior to 1982 the Commandos had been composed largely of volunteers.

However, the self-image of the noble Afrikaner, gun in hand defending the Volk, was being seriously undermined by the undermanning of these Commandos. In 1982, on average Commando units had only 60% of their required manpower. In some of the more vital border areas the situation was even worse, with border depopulation leading to some Commandos having only 5% of their required manpower (Thabazimbi on the Botswana border, for example).[5] The state of the Commandos became so bad that from 1979 an increasing number of conscripted national servicemen had to be allocated to the Commandos to bolster their volunteer strength.

It is in the Commandos that the bulk of Community citizens and those eligible for Community citizenship will be drawn into the defence of Apartheid, for it is the Commandos which within the Apartheid regime's concept of "area defence" provide the first line of defence for the suppression of internal resistance. It is to the Commandos that area protection falls, freeing the Permanent Force and Citizen Force for a more offensive role.

The central role of the Commandos in the defence of Apartheid was laid out by the then Commander in chief of the SADF Constand Viljoen in 1982:

"They (the ANC) are going to fight an area war... If we had to deal with this using the full-time force, the demands on the system would be too great. But we are going to deal with it by using Area Defence ... people living in the area must be organised to defend themselves. They must be our first line of defence. Our full-time force must be a reaction force. The first line of defence will contain any terrorist threat and the better equipped and trained reaction forces will deal with insurgents."[6]

13

(5) M. Evans, 'Restructuring: The Role of the Military' in South Africa Review (Raven Press 1983), p. 45.
(6) G. Cawthra, Brutal Force (IDAF 1986), p. 229.

OFFICIAL SADF BREAKDOWN OF THE COMPOS

14   *Source: Star 8.11.82*

Urban Commandos which can consist of two elements

An area protection force	A reaction force

Tasks:
- Supporting the SA Police with regard to hearth and home protection.
- Protection of National Key Points which do not have their own Industrial Commandos.
- Protection of vulnerable points.
- Intelligence.
- COIN action.
- Supporting of Reaction Forces.
- Assistance to civilian authorities.

Tasks:
COIN operations in support of the SA Police, including:
- Roadblocks.
- Cordons.
- Searches.
- Crowd control
- Curfew arrangements

ON AND ROLE OF THE COMMANDO FORCE

Rural Commandos which can consist of two elements

Industrial Commandos (only at National Key Points)

An area protection force

A reaction force

Tasks:
• Hearth and home protection.
• Protection of National Key Points which do not have their own Industrial Commandos.
• Intelligence
• COIN action.
• Support to the SA Police.
• Assistance to civilian authorities.

Tasks:
• Immediate support to the SA Police.
• Pursuit of the enemy.
• Patrolling.
• Strengthening the area protection force.

Tasks:
• Protection of National Key Points against terrorist attacks.
• Intelligence in respect of the external threat against National Key Points.

The problem for the military chiefs was that male South Africans were not responding in a voluntary manner to the perceived security needs of the state. Many army commanders complained that the average South African male prefers his social life, sport and work above defending their country. According to one army commander cited in the Rand Daily Mail:

"The attitude of the man in the street is that the Defence Force and the Police are responsible for the defence of the country for which they have to pay taxes. So why should they serve in the army?" [7]

In some areas an emergency mobilisation of the Commandos resulted in only 26 of the 218 men turning out, whilst elsewhere national servicemen returning from the operational area in Namibia had to be drafted in as a result of the poor voluntary turn out. [8] Such an unreliable force could hardly constitute the cornerstone of the military's "area defence" strategy, which the SADF leadership put forward publicly in 1982 in response to mounting popular resistance to Apartheid.

2.4 Mounting Resistance: Increased Repression
In 1981, according to the Head of the Security Branch, Major General Steenkamp, there were 55 military actions carried out by the ANC, nearly three times the 1980 level. [9] In 1981 workers' strikes and student militancy increased, whilst in the face of SWAPO's ongoing liberation struggle General Magnus Malan admitted in Parliament that:

"the number of troops deployed in the various operational areas in South West Africa (Namibia) and South Africa increased by more than 5,000% between 1975 and 1981." [10]

It was furthermore revealed that over the next three years South Africa intended to increase its military presence in Namibia, thereby placing further demands on the SADF's manpower resources. This mounting resistance and increased repression in both Namibia and South Africa seriously overstretched the SADF's existing manpower resources. As a result it became essential to draw into the active defence of Apartheid a larger number of white South African males.

In 1982 the Defence Amendment Act was passed. This act extended the period of service in the Citizen Force after two years of national service to twelve years, involving in alternate years three months and one month camps. It furthermore extended conscription into the Commandos. This affected older white men (between 30 and 55) who had missed the call up in the 1950s and 1960s. This measure made available an extra 800,000 men for conscription, doubling the existing

(7) Rand Daily Mail, 24.3.82. (8) ibid. (9) G. Cawthra, op. cit., p. 217. (10) ibid., p. 229.

number potentially available for conscription. It was this Act which extended active participation in the defence of Apartheid to the bulk of male European citizens resident in South Africa who hold dual nationality. At the time a SADF spokesman declared:

"We will not be taking 800,000 men out of the economy. What we are trying to do is keep the men involved in the economy while they do military service. A farmer, for example, could go home after doing eight hours of duty. A businessman will report for duty at times which will enable him to continue his business activity." [11]

What this amounted to was a declaration that as a matter of routine all adult male South Africans would be required to bear arms in defence of Apartheid. From the spring of 1984, as resistance to Apartheid has escalated so European citizens have increasingly been thrown into the frontline in defence of Apartheid. (The reality of this deadly daily war will be illustrated in later sections.)

ESCALATING CONSCRIPTION

1957 Defence Amendment Act
Conscription by ballot system introduced.

1967 Compulsory System
9 months national service introduced for all young white men.

1972
Conscription extended to 12 months, with Citizen Force camps of 19 days per annum for five years.

1975
Emergency 3 month tours introduced for the Citizen Force. These have become a permanent feature of military service.

1982 Defence Amendment Act
Citizen Force participation extended to 12 years with three month and one month camps in alternate years. Conscription into the Commandos extended to older white men who missed the call up in the 1950s and 1960s. Commandos become cornerstone of the area defence strategy.

1984 South African Citizenship Amendment Act
This introduced greater compulsion towards immigrants on the question of taking out South African citizenship and brought 46,000 immigrants into the National Service net.

(11) Rand Daily Mail, 25.3.82.

September 1984
Border duty extended from three months to six months at a stretch for
national servicemen.

June 1985
Citizen Force call up of one month extended to two months with mounting
popular resistance.

GROWTH OF S.A.FORCES

	1977	1979	1981	1983	1985	1987
PF	28,000	40,000	50,000	55,000	60,000	65,000
NSM	27,000	60,000	62,000	65,000	65,000	65,000
CF	180,000	230,000	280,000	330,000	360,000	360,000
Cdos	120,000	150,000	140,000	160,000	280,000	400,000
Civils	12,500	14,000	15,000	16,000	17,000	18,000
TOTAL	**367,000**	**494,000**	**547,000**	**626,000**	**772,000**	**908,000**

ESTIMATED PERSONNEL STRENGTH – NOTES:

1. **1977 & 1979**: Figures are from IDAF's publication, 'The Apartheid War
   Machine', p. 41.

2. **PF**: Permanent Force – 1979 to 1981 increase was result of formation of black
   tribal units and mercenary recruitment, mainly from Zimbabwe. PF strength
   will continue to increase gradually with recruitment of blacks and white
   women. This recruitment programme is likely to be less successful than
   presently anticipated by SADF.

3. **NSM**: National Service – Annual intake of white male NS men will level out at
   about 32,500 a year. Two years' service means there are twice this number
   in service at any one time. This table does not take into account the
   possible conscription of white women and rules out the possibility of black
   conscription before 1983.

4. **CF**: Citizen Force – Under the new 12 year service conditions the CF will
   absorb about 30,000 conscripts who have completed their national service
   each year (This allows for about 2,500 to be transferred to the Commandos
   by their own request). CF strength will level out at about 360,000 – that is, 12
   intakes of 30,000. After this number entering the CF each year will
   approximate the number leaving who have completed their commitments.

5. **Cdos**: Commandos – According to the SADF there are 800,000 potential conscripts for Commandos. It wil not be practically possible to absorb all these people at a rapid rate. The estimates given represent a gradual absorption of new members.

6. **Civils**: Civilians in SADF employment – the numbers will go up as the larger military machine requires more administrative staff.

19

(Source: Resister no. 19, April-May 1982)

.5 The Impact on the Immigrant Community

In the past some migrants to South Africa waited until they passed the age of 25 before applying for South African citizenship, military conscription. This caused considerable resentment amongst those South African citizens who as a result had to carry the main burden of conscription. It was in order to draw a larger number of foreign nationals (who also enjoyed South African citizenship) into the defence of Apartheid that the 1982 Defence Amendment Act was passed.

Under this act older men who had never done military service before were required to do 30 days training in the first year, followed by a maximum of 12 days per annum until the age of 55. This drew an extra 800,000 white males into the pool available for service in the Commandos, of which a substantial number enjoyed European citizenship on a dual nationality basis. Men from this pool would be called up if the local situation warranted it to man area defence systems against guerrilla attacks or other forms of resistance. This concept of area defence had been formulated in the face of increasingly effective resistance to Apartheid. According to General Viljoen the ANC's 'area war' would strain the available manpower and area defence offered the only solution if the Permanent Force and National Service Conscripts were not to be frittered away on guard duties throughout the country.[12] Indeed, according to Robert Jaster, as South Africa has moved onto a war footing since 1975 manpower constraints have been such that the Defence Force was unable to establish a Permanent Force Brigade to serve as the SADF's basic force in being.[13] This may have served to constrain South Africa's aggression against the independent states of the region.

In 1983, Minister of Defence Malan estimated that every active soldier required infrastructural support from 7 other military personnel[14]; it was the hope that these administrative duties could increasingly be devolved to Commando Force personnel. It is through this releasing of

(12) Financial Mail, 2.4.82.   (13) ibid.   (14) cited in G. Cawthra, op. cit., p. 117.

Permanent Force and National Service soldiers for more active duties that the participation of European citizens in the Commandos is making a major contribution to South Africa's repeated invasions of Angola; destabilisation of the region; continued occupation of Namibia and since 1984 heightened repression in the townships of South Africa itself. Thus it can be seen that behind the comic image of a 'Dad's Army' lies a serious and deadly intent which ensures that European citizens actively contribute to the perpetuation of Apartheid.

In 1984 European citizens were further embroiled in the defence of Apartheid through the South African Citizenship Amendment Act. This Act (see inset) increased the level of compulsion on young foreign nationals between the ages of 15 and 25 to take out South African citizenship with its concomitant obligation to do compulsory military service. In 1984 close on IO% of South Africa's whites were not citizens of South Africa. Of the 475,000 whites who were resident in the country but who were not citizens 24,700 were West Germans; 9,200 were Greeks, 18,000 were Italians, 20,500 Dutch, 49,400 Portuguese; 226,900 British and 28,400 other Europeans, a total of some 377,100 citizens of the Community.[15]

EUROPEANS IN THE SADF

Assuming the same age and sex distribution amongst European citizenship holders as amongst the general white South African population, and assuming the 1984 legislation compelled only 75% of non-citizens to take out South African citizenship, then one can calculate the numbers of European Community (EC) citizens affected by the different categories of military obligation.* The National Service and Commando obligations laid on white males affect respectively 13.5% and 20.3% of the total white population. Thus we would expect to find the following numbers from various citizenship holding groups affected by the various military service obligations:

	Holding both EC and SA citizenship	18-32 Age Group National Service	32-55 Age Group Commando Service
UK	443,575	59,883	90,046
Portugal	587,650	79,333	119,293
Germany	93,825	12,666	19,046
Italy	45,500	6,143	9,237
Holland	34,875	4,708	7,080
Belgium	25,000	3,375	5,075
France	8,000	1,080	1,624
Greece	77,700	10,490	15,773
Ireland	2,400	324	487
	1,318,525	178,002	267,661

(15) Star, 22.2.85.

As the inset on p. 21 shows there is a category of South Africans approximately numbering 732,600 that is eligible to a British, Dutch or Irish citizenship. This category is affected by military service obligations as well, possibly adding the following numbers of Europeans affected:

	Holding SA and eligible to EC citizenship	18-32 Age Group National Service	32-55 Age Group Commando Service
UK	500,000	67,500	101,500
Holland	160,000	21,600	32,480
Ireland	72,600	9,801	14,738
	732,600	98,901	148,718

* *Given migration patterns (younger people, predominantly male), immigrants that arrived in the past 25 years are likely to have a different age and sex distribution to the South African population as a whole (i.e. more males of working age in the immigrant community). As a result our calculations are likely to be an underestimation of the number of European citizens involved in each category of military service.*

The 75% estimate gives figures which approximate statements on the overall impact of the 1984 measures by the South African military. The distribution between different European nationalities may not be proportional however.

It was estimated that the extension of citizenship entailed in the South African Citizenship Amendment Act would make at least an extra 46,000 men eligible for conscription into the SADF almost immediately.[16] This is equivalent to one and a half times the annual national service intake.

In January 1985 the first batch of immigrants eligible for conscription under the 1984 legislation were drafted into the SADF and it was announced that all immigrant males liable for national service under the provisions of the 1984 Act would be called up for their first initial training period within the coming year (which included the July 1985 and January 1986 call ups). This was in the words of Defence Minister Malan, the "small price to pay for the privilege of living in South Africa".[17]

2.6 Fighting for Apartheid: A Job for Life
What would the life of a 18 year old European citizen look like following his acceptance of South African citizenship and conscription into the SADF?

(16) Assuming a proportional representation amongst the nationalities of non-South African citizens, this would bring an extra 36,525 European citizenship holders into the SADF (of 475,000 non-citizens 377,100 EC citizens or some 79.4%) (17) cited in the Cape Times, 23.2.82.

SA Citizenship automatic by naturalisation

If you are living in the Republic of South Africa on permanent resident permits, this brochure contains important information *affecting you personally,* with regard to:

- the automatic acquistion of *South African citizenship*

- your *National Service obligations* when you become South African citizens.

Three groups are affected.

1. Persons to whom permanent resident permits were issued before 19 April 1978.

In terms of Section 11A of the South African Citizenship Act 1949 (Act 44 of 1949), amended by the South African Citizenship Amendment Act (Act 43 of 1984), as published in the Government Gazette of 11 April 1984, those persons who on 11 October 1984:

- a. are in the age group 15 years 6 months to 25 years
- b. received their permanent resident before 19 April 1978
- c. have been ordinarily resident in the Republic of South Africa for a period of at least five years,

will automatically become South African citizens by naturalisation on that date.

2. Persons to whom permanent resident permits were issued between the period 19 April 1978 to 10 April 1982.

Persons in this category fall within the provisions Section 11A of Act 44 of 1949 as it existed immediately prior to the amendment which came into force on 11 April 1984. They automatically became South African Citizens before or on the 10 April 1984 if on that date they were not older than 23 years and had been ordinarily resident in the Republic of South Africa for at least two years.

3. Persons to whom permanent resident permits have been issued since 11 April 1982.

Persons in this category will automatically become South African citizens by naturalisation if they are not younger than 15 years 6 months and not older than 25 years on the day they have been ordinarily resident in South Africa for five years.

National Service Commitments

In terms of the Defence Act (Act 44 of 1957) these new male citizens will be liable for National Service. They are also obliged to register for National Service within 30 days of becoming citizens. Those who are still at school may obtain the registration forms at their schools. Others must write to the Registering Officer at:

The Registering Officer
Private Bag X281
Pretoria
0001

Telephone : (012) 323 8911 or 323 9151.

In January 1985 he would begin two years full-time national service, during which time he would probably serve at least one six-month tour of duty in an "operational area", in northern Namibia/southern Angola or along South Africa's borders. Alternatively, he might be allocated to serve with the South African Police, which increasingly carries out para-military functions.

Having survived his two years national service (which is by no means a foregone conclusion, with some 250 National Servicemen dying through "accidents" each year and the rate of attempted suicide amongst conscripts increasing 17 fold in two years, to 429 in 1986), from January 1987 he would be a member of the Citizen Force for 12 more years during which time he would be expected to perform a full 720 days of service, This would be split between, in alternate years, camps of 90 days and 30 days duration, during which time he will once again see active service in an operational area, be it in Namibia or southern Angola, along the border or in the townships.
In 1999, at the age of 32 he would be transferred for five years to the active Citizen Force Reserve, where he would be called up as required for up to a further 120 days service every two years.
In 2004, at the age of 37 he would be transferred to the Commandos, where he would provide 12 days service per year until he reached the age of 55. On 1 January 2023, he would be transferred to the National Reserve, from which, if the situation warranted it, he could be called up once again to bear arms in defence of Apartheid. In 2033 he would finally find himself free from any commitment to bear arms in defence of Apartheid. In June 1986 the Commonwealth Eminent Persons Group (EPG) submitted its report on South Africa; it concluded that:

"once decisions involving greater violence are made on both sides, they carry an inevitability of their own and are difficult, if not impossible to reverse, except as a result of exhaustion through prolonged conflict".[18]

It then went on to speak of the possibility of South Africa witnessing "the worst bloodbath since the Second World War".[19]
In 2033 our European citizen, having been a party to this scenario, and having paid the small price of 15.6% of his life in armed defence of Apartheid "for the privilege of living in South Africa"[20], could leave his ravaged land and return to Europe where he will enjoy all the benefits accorded to citizens of Europe.

2.7 The Extent of Business Support for the SADF

7.1 Protection of National (Industrial) Key Points
The SADF is not merely an armed defender of the territorial sovereignty

(18) Mission to South Africa: The Commonwealth Report (Commonwealth Secretariat), p. 67-68.

(19) ibid.   (20) Magnus Malan cited in the Cape Times, 23.2.82.

of South Africa. The SADF is an explicit supporter and defender of Apartheid. Not only is the SADF firmly committed to the government's policy of Apartheid but it is now also a major force in government policy formulation through its participation in the State Security Council.

Not only are individual white European citizens in South Africa a bastion of support for the SADF but also domestic South African and transnational corporations are extensively enmeshed in the repressive machinery which has been built up to crush popular resistance to Apartheid.

As ANC President Oliver Tambo pointed out to Business International in May 1987:

"All companies in South Africa, including multinationals and subsidiaries of foreign concerns, are integrated into Pretoria's strategic planning and directly into the repressive machinary. This is done institutionally by their participation on committees and boards, by complying with legislation and by financial and other support." [21]

In addition to paying taxes and purchasing Defence Bonds businesses are principally (though by no means solely) embroiled in the military defence of Apartheid through the National Key Points Act 1980. This Act empowered the Minister of Defence to declare any place or area a Key Point; to compel its owners to implement, at their own expense, security precautions as laid down by a government committee; and to prohibit publication of any information regarding security measures at a Key Point. Owners who failed to comply with the regulations faced prison sentences of up to 5 years and fines of up to R20,000.

Initially there was some resistance to the Key Points Act from companies which baulked at being forced to pay for 'services' they regarded as the responsibility of government, but the South African monolith which the government wishes to create in defence of Apartheid, would not be denied and opposition soon waned. Despite the fears of some foreign owned companies that their increased involvement with the SADF and SAP entailed in the provisions of the Key Points Act would lead to accusations that they were openly collaborating in the armed defence of Apartheid, within a few months 85% of the 633 identified Key Points were fully cooperating with the government.

The importance of the provisions embodied in the Key Points Act was spelt out by the then head of the SADF Lt-General Constand Viljoen at the Pelindaba Nuclear Installation in 1980:

(21) 'South Africa at the Crossroads', Speeches delivered in May 1987 by President Tambo to Business International, (ANC Lusaka).

"It is essential that industrial commandos should be raised as soon as possible so that part-time soldiers can assume responsibility for territorial defence. This will leave the regular forces for operations such as border protection and strikes at enemy bases." [22]

A confidential memorandum leaked from General Motors revealed that these industrial commandos would be placed under direct army command in the event of an "emergency". [23]

In many respects the Key Points Act merely formalised a relationship which had been in existence for some time. A government Committee of Inquiry into Riots on the Mines as early as 1976 was making recommendations on the security of these vital Key Points. These recommendations included the suggestion that every mine should have a properly trained security unit equipped with patrol dogs, teargas, batons and where possible an armoured vehicle, and that furthermore this unit should "practice regularly with units of surrounding mines and with the South African Police." This and the other recommendations were put into force during the 1970s, before such obligations were statutorily laid on companies through the Key Points Act.

Foreign Companies frequently willingly complied with these types of government recommendations in order to prove themselves good corporate citizens and in order to ensure that they continued to enjoy the high profits which the labour repressive system of Apartheid allows. As resistance to Apartheid mounted however, a number of foreign companies feared the implications for their other concerns of too close an identification with the repressive side of their South African investments. As a result in 1984 the Key Points Act was amended to allow outside firms to guard Key Points sites. This enables the companies concerned to distance themselves from brutality exercised on their behalf by security forces in the suppression of workers' protest actions and strikes.

7.2 *Voluntary Supplementary Payments For Conscripted White Employees*
Foreign companies wish to appear 'neutral' in their involvement in South Africa and often stress the benefits to black workers arising from their operations. European companies are however heavily embroiled in the military defence of Apartheid. This is not just through the Key Points Act and the obligations which this lays on them to set up industrial commandos and large security forces, but also through their direct wage subsidies to the SADF. The vast majority of foreign companies on a voluntary basis make "top-up payments" to white employees called up to perform national service obligations. This represents a major subsidy from the private sector to the SADF and its absence would lead

(22) Resister No. 50, June-July 1987.
(23) UN Centre Against Apartheid, Notes and Documents 12/84, August 1984.

either to additional financial burdens on the state or to considerable dissatisfaction amongst conscripts (who would have to take a drop in income as a result of their military commitments). At the time of the 1982 extension of the call up a number of business representatives questioned whether employers could afford to continue with top-up pay, if this were extended by an additional two or three months a year. They nevertheless continued to do so.

These supplementary payments to white employees to fight in armed defence of Apartheid contrast markedly with corporate treatment of black employees who may be detained for their opposition to the injustices of Apartheid. These black detainees receive no top-up pay, in fact they receive no pay at all. Their families receive no subsistance allowance. Instead they are almost automatically sacked, regardless of the suffering this may bring upon them and their dependants. Such is the 'neutrality' of European companies operating in South Africa.

A further major area of European corporate involvement in defence of Apartheid lies in their extensive involvement in the Apartheid regime's efforts to achieve self-sufficiency in the sphere of armaments production. Despite significant innovations over the years in the face of the international arms embargo the fact remains that the Apartheid regime could not maintain its current level of armaments without the collaboration of western companies, many of which are European. In this manner such household names as Marconi, Plessey, Philips, AEG-Telefunken, Siemens, BP and ICI are involved in sustaining the military capacity of the SADF to wage war in defence of Apartheid throughout the Southern African region.

WAGE SUBSIDY TO THE SADF: A BASIS FOR CALCULATION

Given the military obligations laid on the 18-55 male age group (18-20 full-time military service; 20-32 an average of 60 days per year military service; 32-55 an average of 9 days per year military service) and the fact that companies pay top-up pay to employees called up, one can calculate the wage subsidy to the SADF this constitutes.

In 1985:
20-32 age group constitutes 25.0% EAP   (Economically Active Population)
32-55 age group constitutes 44.2% EAP

20-32 age group on average spend 16.6% of working time doing military service
32-55 age group on average spend 6.7% of working time doing military service.

This implies a loss of 4.15% of total white male waged labour time from the 20-32 age group and a loss of 3.0% of total waged labour time from the 32-55 age group. Giving a total loss of 7.15% of total waged labour time from the EAP as a result of military service obligations in the SADF.

Given existing pay scales for South African servicemen and assuming that the majority of conscripts remain as ordinary soldiers, then the average daily pay would be Rand 12. This would give an annual income of R4,380. Taking the average white wage in European companies to be approximately R21,000* then top-up payments by European companies to conscripts would be 80% of their normal pay. This would mean that fully 5.72% of the white male wage bill goes as a wage subsidy to the SADF.

This would mean that for every white male South African citizen employed by a European company a wage subsidy of some R1,201 per annum would be paid to the SADF.

The number of white South African citizens employed by European companies can be estimated by using the 1988 report on the EC Code of Conduct (period until 30.6.86).**
Non-black labour accounts for 31,048 employees in companies from Belgium, Denmark, Germany, Greece, Spain, France, the Netherlands and Portugal. Taking into account personnel on secondment, female and coloured labour, the male white force will be 18,629 (60%). This would lead to an annual wage subsidy supporting the SADF of R22,373,188 (ECU 10,123,867).
Italian and (mainly) British companies employ 75% of the total number of black labour hired by European companies. The Code of Conduct-report however does not give non-black labour employed in British and Italian companies. When the proportion of black and non-black labour is assumed to be the same in British and Italian as in other EC companies, then a further 93,123 non-blacks were hired by EC companies in South Africa. This might lead to a further 55,874 male whites in EC companies, and a further annual subsidy to the SADF of R67,104,433 (ECU 30,364,755).
In practical terms, this means that European companies from Belgium, Denmark, Germany, Greece, Spain, France, the Netherlands and Portugal together subsidise an equivalent of 1332 full-time South African soldiers. European companies from (mainly) the UK and Italy may subsidise a further equivalent of 3994 full-time soldiers.

*   In 1986 the average white industrial wage was R21,252. It is assumed that most European investment is concentrated in the manufacturing sector (or the equally highly paid mining sector), hence the round figure of Rand 21,000 is used. In 1986 the average value of the Rand was .4525 ECU.

** See document PE 121.496 of 12.4.88. This number will be a serious underestimation, as a 1984 UN study suggests that more then half of the EC companies, especially those from the UK and Germany, do not report.

2.8 The Response of the Business Community To the Extension of Conscription.

The attitude of the South African business community to the extension of the call up embodied in the 1982 legislation was summed up by Mr Vincent Brett, the Chairman of the Management Committee of the Association of Chambers of Commerce (ASSCOM) who observed:

"The extended call up means that men who have a lot of experience in the business world will be called up. The loss of these men to the business world even for short periods could cause problems. Unfortunately the men who are valuable to the private sector might also be most valuable to the army." [24]

ASSCOM was principally concerned about the severe economic consequences which could result from an extended call up, as was the Afrikaans Handelsinstituut (its Afrikaans-speaking equivalent), which called on the government to ensure that the private sector was disrupted as little as possible by the new measures.

When conscription was extended to bring in immigrants through the 1984 South African Citizenships Amendment Act, the South African government sought to meet the concerns of the business community over skill shortages in specific sectors by introducing a new five-year temporary residence permit.
Addressing the South African–German Chamber of Trade and Industry the then Home Affairs Minister F.W. De Klerk explained how the new temporary residence permit would allow key personnel to work in South Africa for five years without their children being liable for military service. This measure was introduced specifically to calm the fears of personnel on secondment from international corporations to South African subsidiaries.

No one in the business community voiced doubts about the long term implications for South African society of the extension of the call up, which represented a decision by the South African government to use greater violence in defence of Apartheid. This was left to the liberal press. The Daily News described the extended call up as

"the most depressing admission of failure the South African government has yet had to make." [25]

(24) Star, 14.11.82. (25) Daily News (Editorial), 24.3.82.

Indeed, as the Financial Mail commented,

"Short of a political solution to South Africa's problems the SADF's case for an extended call up is compelling."[26]

This seems to have been borne out by subsequent events, as the Apartheid regime continues to face the most sustained challenge to its domination ever mounted by the non-racial democratic opposition. Since early 1984, the black townships of South Africa have sought to throw off the administrative hand of Apartheid structures, and with some 35,372 soldiers being deployed in the townships in 1985 alone in an attempt to break popular resistance, European citizens have become increasingly embroiled on a daily basis in confrontations with black youths.[27]

(26) Financial Mail, 2.4.82.   (27) Resister No. 44, June/July 1986.

EUROPEANS IN THE SADF: A DIFFERENT KIND OF WAR

3.1 Namibia: Africa's Last Colony

In 1920, following imperial Germany's defeat in the First World War the German colony of South West Africa (Namibia) was placed under a League of Nations mandate, to be administered by South Africa on behalf of the British Crown. Following the Second World War the South African government, which had to all intents and purposes administered Namibia as a fifth province of South Africa, refused to hand over the mandate for Namibia to the United Nations, on the grounds that it did not recognise the UN as the successor of the League of Nations in this regard.

In 1950, following petitions to the UN by Namibians, the International Court of Justice (ICJ) unanimously decided that the mandate was still in existence. This had no impact on the South African government, which continued to implement its grand Apartheid strategy for Namibia, essentially based on ethnically defined homelands for black Namibians. In 1960 the South West African People's Organisation (SWAPO) was formed and in 1965 it was recognised by the Organisation of African Unity (OAU) as the liberation movement of Namibia. In 1966 the UN General Assembly revoked South Africa's mandate over Namibia and ordered South Africa to withdraw. The South African government paid no attention to this revocation of its legal basis for administering Namibia and refused to withdraw. As a result SWAPO was left with no alternative but to launch a liberation war to force South Africa to terminate its illegal occupation of Namibia.

In 1971 the ICJ gave an advisory opinion which unequivocally declared South Africa's occupation of Namibia illegal. In consequence it called upon all UN Member States to refrain from any dealings with South Africa which implied recognition of its presence in Namibia. The British government took the view that while acknowledging the illegality of South Africa's occupation, it was nevertheless free to accept that de facto South Africa was the administering authority. This British position represented de facto acceptance of South Africa's illegal occupation of Namibia, and can in large part be held to be representative of the stance adopted by the Community as a whole.

Since 1975, following the collapse of Portuguese colonial rule in Angola and Mozambique, Namibia has become a land occupied on a scale comparable with Nazi-Germany's 1940 occupation of western Europe. Troop deployments in Namibia rose from 16,000 to 50,000[28] as northern Namibia was used as a base for the invasion of Angola in an attempt to install a compliant UNITA/FNLA regime in Luanda.

White Namibians with South African citizenship – the vast majority of the whites – have been conscripted in the same way as white South Africans. The provisions of the 1982 legislation were extended to Namibia in 1984, and registration in some magisterial districts implemented. In an attempt to "Namibianise" the war conscription for black Namibians was introduced in 1980. This has led to the establishment of the South West African Territory Force (SWATF), which although nominally separate remains de facto an integral part of the SADF, with the commmand structure of the SWATF largely being run by SADF personnel "on secondment".

In 1985 the commander of the South African occupying forces acknowledged that there were 40,000 SADF and SWATF troops "on the Angolan border"[29], the implication being that this figure excluded troops in support roles outside of the "Operational Areas" which straddle the border. All in all it seems likely that some l00,000 troops controlled by South Africa now occupy Namibia, a ratio of 1 Soldier to every 14 civilians.[30] With the extension of the call up to European immigrants it seems likely that an increasing number of European citizens will be involved in this illegal occupation. More than a quarter of the white population in Namibia are believed to enjoy rights to West German citizenship and many of these have been conscripted into the defence of South Africa's illegal occupation. This involvement merely extends the role of European citizens in the illegal occupation of Namibia.
European citizens have since 1975 been involved in fighting for the SADF in the occupation of Namibia and in South Africa's forward policy which has involved repeated invasions of Angola and since August 1981 the virtually continuous occupation of southern Angola.

On 29 January 1981 a British citizen, Trevor Edwards deserted the SADF and described to the British newspaper The Guardian the brutal reality in which European citizens participated in northern Namibia and southern Angola:

"Some of it is pretty heavy. Sometimes we take the locals for questioning. It's rough. We just beat them, cut them, burn them. As soon as we're finished with them, we kill them. We've got Angolan government soldiers and taken them back to base for proper questioning.

(28) G. Cawthra, op. cit., p. 181.
(29) ibid., p. 178.   (30) ibid

Sometimes you have to do it to the children to make the adults talk. There was a twelve year old boy. We wanted to know what was going on. We wanted his mother to talk, so we tied him up like a chicken with his wrists up behind his back, strapped to his ankles. Then we played water polo with him, put him in this kind of dam and pushed him about, let him sink. Every so often we took him out. He wouldn't cry. He just wet himself. The mother didn't tell us anything. In the end we just left him in the water and he drowned... When it comes to killing women hanging them and things there are some of them who laugh about it. They take photographs of themselves with bodies. They don't see them as people just as things that are there." [31]

Offensives launched by the South African Army across the country's borders proved more effective than playing a waiting game... Giving statistics on the casualty rate General Geldenhuys said on average one civilian or member of the armed forces died for every 14 terrorists killed in defensive actions. In across the border initiatives the ratio was 1:38. "In terms of human life it is more economical to launch offensive actions than for us to sit and wait for terrorists to attack us", he emphasized.
The Star (SA) 26.3.82

Edwards had moved from the Rhodesian Army to the 32 Battalion of the SADF in 1980. Towards the end of that year Edwards finally experienced an incident which thoroughly unnerved him and prompted his desertion. Edwards was leading his platoon through the bush of southern Angola in search of SWAPO guerrillas whose trail they'd picked up when suddenly they were confronted by two small children, Edwards himself takes up the story:

"I said: 'Don't shoot them'. There was one of our guys who started shouting to them in the local language. Then these other kids popped up and started to run as well, so obviously I said: 'Put them out'. We started shooting. More and more of them kept jumping up and running. Some of them were completely naked. They'd taken their clothes off to show they weren't armed. We shot this young girl. She must have been about five. And we shot her father. We shot about nine in all.
I don't know how, but somehow this girl's mother and her sister didn't get shot. Well, we left them there and carried on with our patrol, moving on in box formation. She followed us: this mother and her little kid. She followed us all day, just walked about 100 metres behind us. She didn't cry or say anything. Every time we stopped, she stopped. We went back and tried to shoo her away, but she just came back and followed us. This freaked me out. Every time you turned round, she was there. It started me thinking." [32]

(31) Guardian, 29.1.1981.
(32) Guardian, 29.1.81.

Apart from its effect on Edwards the incident was pure routine for the South African forces operating in Namibia and Angola. Such brutalities and atrocities are commonplace in both Angola and Namibia. The 1982 report of the Southern African Catholic Bishops Conference on Namibia described the situation in northern Namibia as follows:

"It is commonly accepted that in searching out SWAPO guerrillas the Security Forces stop at nothing to force information out of people. They break into homes, beat up residents, shoot people, steal and kill cattle and often pillage stores and tea rooms. When the tracks of SWAPO guerrillas are discovered by the Security Forces the local people are in danger. Harsh measures are intensified. People are blindfolded, taken from their homes and left beaten up and even dead by the roadside. Women are often raped. It is not unknown for a detachment to break into a home and while black soldiers keep watch over the family, white soldiers select the best-looking girls and take them into the veld to rape them. There is no redress because reporting irregularities or atrocities to commanders is considered a dangerous and fruitless exercise." [33]

Prior to 1985 European citizens voluntarily and routinely participated in these atrocities either through directly volunteering for service in the SADF or by taking out South African citizenship.

Since 1985 the net for conscription has been cast even wider, bringing in even more European citizens into routine participation in atrocities in Angola and Namibia.

A 19 year-old British citizen, who volunteered to do national service in the SADF, has been killed in an accidental explosion in the operational area in Namibia. Rifleman Mark John Littrell had four months of his service to complete when he was killed last Saturday. A SADF spokesman confirmed the death but declined to comment on the nature of the explosion or whether any other people were injured.
The Star 8.8.85

3.2 The SADCC Region: South Africa's Destructive Engagement.

Coinciding with the independence of Zimbabwe in 1980 the 9 majority-ruled states of Southern Africa came together to form the Southern African Development Coordination Conference (SADCC). The European Community played an important role in supporting this regional economic initiative, which aimed both to reduce the region's excessive economic dependence on South Africa and to promote regional economic development. The immediate international support which the

(33) South African Catholic Bishops Conference Report on Namibia 1982.

SADCC garnered, coupled with the euphoria surrounding the independence of Zimbabwe, held out the promise of peace and a new beginning for the hard-pressed countries of Southern Africa.

This mood of euphoria was brutally broken on the night of 30 January 1981 when a unit of the SADF stole into the Maputo suburb of Matola and shot dead 12 South African refugees and a Portuguese technician, Jose Antonio Monteiro. As the South African forces withdrew from Matola they left behind not only equipment emblazoned with Nazi insignia but also one of their number, who had been killed in the raid. Shortly afterwards the body was identified as that of Sergeant Robert Lewis Hutchinson, a British citizen.

Hutchinson had initially served in the Security Forces of the Smith regime in Rhodesia and after 1980 had signed up in the SADF. The British government's only response to Hutchinson's death in Maputo in the service of the SADF was to request, on behalf of the family, that Hutchinson's body be delivered to the British government. On humanitarian grounds the Mozambican government consented to do so and reiterated its appeal to all governments to:

"take effective action against the recruitment, transport and protection of mercenaries" [34]

The raid on Matola was to signal the beginning of South Africa's intensive campaign of destabilisation against the SADCC region, designed to maintain the region's dependence on South Africa. In the following months the actions of South Africa's surrogate forces in Mozambique and Angola were increasingly directed at the region's transportation and communications infrastructure. On occasion the sophistication of these actions led to speculation about a more direct South African involvement. In Mozambique, surrogate forces launched a generalised reign of terror against the rural population, whilst in Angola the SADF began its occupation of the South.

In the face of this aggression the SADCC sought to enlist international support in its condemnation of South Africa, but both the United Kingdom and the Federal Republic of Germany (along with the United States and the World Bank) refused to endorse the final communiqué of the second SADCC International Consultative Conference, held in Blantyre, Malawi in November 1981, which specifically condemned South Africa's actions.

What lay behind this condemnation was a series of attacks against transportation targets immediately prior to the Conference, including the

(34) AIM Bulletin, January 1981.

Pungwe river bridge along the Beira-Mutare railway and the harbour buoys in Beira harbour, which interrupted the flow of traffic between Beira and Malawi (traffic between Beira and Zimbabwe was already disrupted following the attack on the Pungwe bridge). On 21 October 1981 a Mozambican army unit guarding the Beira Corridor happened upon a group of men planting mines on the railway line. They fired a bazooka at the group blowing up four men. A white ear was found nearby along with a kit-bag containing a half-finished novel about Northern Ireland. This constituted clear evidence of non-Mozambican involvement, with the evidence strongly suggesting South African involvement in the sabotage of the region's transportation infrastructure.

South Africa's war of destabilisation continued and on 9 December 1982 the wanton murder of innocent civilians spread to the tiny mountain Kingdom of Lesotho, which is entirely surrounded by South African territory, when the SADF invaded the capital Maseru and killed in cold blood 42 people. The dead included 12 Basotho, including 5 women and 2 children.

In July 1983 the SADCC issued an appeal

"We do not ask that anyone should go to war on our behalf but we do ask that those who claim to be our friends should exercise those constraints which are within their power to force South Africa to desist from its actions." [35]

The type of "constraints" which the SADCC leadership had in mind is aptly illustrated by the fact that on 23 February 1983 the British newspaper The Observer, revealed that the white ear found along the Beira-Mutare railway in October 1981 belonged to Lt Alan Gingles, a British officer from Larne, Northern Ireland, who had been serving in the SADF. In late October 1981 a South African spokesman had announced his death in the "Operational Area" (a term normally used to refer to Namibia). At the time of his death Sandhurst-trained Gingles still held a commission in the British army. The revelation of this fact led the British Defence Minister Michael Heseltine to declare that Lt. Gingles should have asked permission and resigned his commission before joining the SADF. The British government took the opportunity of the Gingles affair to announce that it was not the government's policy to stop former British Army personnel joining the SADF.

It seems somewhat inconsistent that while the British government proudly announces the provision of 109 million of direct bilateral assistance to the SADCC region and its contribution of "substantial funds to transport and communications projects''[36]. British citizens, some of them still holding commissions in the British army, should be allowed actively to engage in sabotaging this same transportation and communications infrastructure.

THE REPORT OF LORNA GUTHRIE, A RED CROSS WORKER IN LESOTHO AT THE TIME OF THE SADF RAID ON MASERU

At one in the morning on December 9 we were woken by the sound of gunfire and mortars. Very soon it was clear that this was a major assault somewhere and the sky was alive with flares.

Because the fighting was so close we did not go to the window to see what we could. But when I heard bullets ricochet off the wall of our house I crept into our baby's room and brought him into our bed. For two hours we lay awake, apprehensive at what such heavy fighting could mean. We heard aircraft and then we knew this must be an external attack on a large scale. Only after sunrise did we emerge to find out if our neighbours and friends were safe. Bullets holes marked the walls of our terrace of houses. A spent mortar shell had crashed through the roof of the house two doors away where a Finnish couple lived. The shell landed a few feet from their bed. It was later identified as being of the type used by the SADF.

We heard that the target nearest to our house was some 300 yards away. I walked there to find 2 people around the house standing silent and stunned. The body of a man who was killed had been taken to the mortuary by his family. The car had been burned and the house ransacked. There was nothing anyone could do, yet they could not leave the scene: yesterday this had been the home of a friend. With a feeling of horror I went across town to some of the other houses which had been destroyed in the raid. A group of people surrounded one house which at first looked untouched.

Then I noticed that the windows were broken and the frames charred. Inside, smoke rose from a pile of debris, which included a human hip bone. According to neighbours, the man in the house had been taken by South African soldiers, wrapped in a blanket and set on fire. Then the house had been devastated by an incendiary device. As I went from house to house which had been hit in the raid, I heard more from local people of the events of the previous night.

These are some extracts: A women, seven months pregnant, was admitted to the Queen Elizabeth Hospital in Maseru with gunshot wounds in the abdomen. In one house, a Lesotho man and his wife and their two children were killed. A month before they had moved into the house after a South African refugee had moved out. In another house three young children owed their lives to their thirteen year old sister. She heard the gunfire and mortars and immediately woke the three younger members of her familiy. She made them lie on the floor and put a mattress over them, and then lay on the

(36) British Aid to Southern Africa (FCO 1987).

mattress. When the soldiers came in she was shot and killed. The three younger children were not found, and survived ... In another house soldiers stormed the building and killed the wife. They then went to the bed, pulled back the blankets and found a four year old child alone there. He was shot and killed. The father was then killed in another room.

38

It seems ironic that while European governments commit over $500 million per annum to economic development activities in the countries of Southern Africa, European citizens should be actively engaging in armed aggression against these same countries, resulting in $10,000 million worth of losses between 1980 and 1984 and a further $25,000 million in 1985 and 1986; and that after 1984 the South African Citizenship Amendment Act had brought in a further 45,000 young, mostly European, conscripts to fight in defence of Apartheid throughout Southern Africa.[37]

Given the escalating human and material costs involved in the Apartheid regime's aggression against the region (which has left no country unaffected) the governments of the SADCC have since 1984 increasingly called on the European Community to take effective action to help eliminate Apartheid in South Africa. It was in the hope of securing action in this area that the Front-Line States' Foreign Ministers met with the EC Foreign Ministers in Lusaka in February 1986. Although the FLS failed to get a commitment on sanctions they did get informal assurances, concerning the termination of external support for the MNR in Mozambique, where the human and material costs of destabilisation have been highest. These assurances like the September 1985 commitment to refuse cooperation with South Africa in the military sphere, were not held to extend to the participation of European citizens in the SADF and consequently the participation of European citizens in the destabilisation of the region continued to grow.

As 1988 opened some 9,000 South African troops were engaged in a major battle in southern Angola. Towards the end of 1987 the scale of the South African involvement and the ferocity of the fighting had become such that the South African government could no longer hide from its public the presence of South African troops in southern Angola. As a result for the first time since 1976, Defence Minister Malan publicly acknowledged that South African troops were in Angola fighting in support of UNITA against the Angolan government.

3.3 South Africa: On the Border and In the Rural Areas

With the victory of ZANU-PF in Zimbabwe in 1980 the focus of the struggle for liberation in Southern Africa shifted decisively towards

(37) SADCC Secretariat.

South Africa and Namibia itself. As the 1980s progressed the ANC became much more active in the rural areas of South Africa. By 1982 Defence Minister Malan admitted that the SADF was deployed in certain border areas of the northern Transvaal and Natal on a full-time basis.[38] By September 1983, he had acknowledged that there were over 10,000 South African troops in 3 operational areas guarding South Africa's borders.[39] This excluded the South African Police Counter Insurgency (COIN) units who were regularly rotated in and out of these border operational areas for deployment alongside the SADF units. Indeed, since 1974 the paramilitary COIN operations of the South African Police (SAP) have expanded to such an extent that a system of transferring military conscripts to the police was introduced to alleviate some of the manpower strains on "normal" police activities. It is estimated that in 1987 approximately 20% of the SAP strength is accounted for by special COIN units. The training of these SAP units is indistinguishable from that of the SADF COIN units. Indeed, as has been repeatedly acknowledged by both the Ministry of Defence and the Ministry of Law and Order the deployment of the SAP and SADF forms part of an integrated defence policy.

In border areas and rural areas the actions of the SAP and SADF are increasingly indistinguishable. Perhaps this is why at the end of 1985 the government was able to substitute 6,000 paramilitary police deployed along South Africa's northern border for 6,000 troops, in order that the police units could be deployed in the townships in an attempt to hoodwink both South African and international public opinion into believing that the country was not rapidly sinking into a state of civil war. This interchangeability between police and military units reveals a further area in which European citizens are participating in the armed defence of Apartheid.

The extension of conscription embodied in the 1982 Defence Amendment Act was designed to bring a strengthened Commando system into a frontline role in defence of Apartheid in the rural and border areas, thereby avoiding tying down thousands of regular soldiers in tedious defence duties. However, depopulation in the border areas threatened thoroughly to undermine this 'area defence' strategy. In 1979 the legal basis for forceful measures to reverse this process had already been laid down with the passing of the Density of Population in Designated Areas Act. This Act gave the government almost unlimited powers to stem the flow of whites away from border areas within 50 km of South Africa's northern borders[40]. Initially, the legislation was merely used as a basis for extending financial incentives to border farmers and as a means of attracting potential white settlers to border regions. However these measures proved insufficient, and by 1982 61% of farms

(38) Rand Daily Mail, 3.4.1982. (39) Argus, 30.9.1983. (40) Resister No. 42, February/March 1986.

in some areas were without a white occupier[41]. In May 1982 therefore the Act's compulsory provisions were activated and they compelled new farmers within 10km of the Botswana and Zimbabwean borders to:

occupy their farms for over 300 days a year, or ensure that they are occupied by a white lessee or full-time white manager, maintain farm roads in a usable condition and fences around farms in good order, keep written records of all people living on the farm, inform the Department of Agriculture within 30 days of any change of ownership or occupation.[42]

In June 1983, in terms of the 1982 Defence Amendment Act, registration of all white males between 18 and 25 began in the three rural Commando areas of Nelspruit, Carolina and Piet Retief, which together encircle South Africa's border with Swaziland. By 1984 the process of registration of all adult males for Commando service had been extended to all areas bordering Swaziland, Mozambique and Zimbabwe, affecting 18,000 men in all. By 1985, this had been extended to the Lesotho and Botswana border areas, and by 1987 with mounting urban resistance it had been extended to large parts of the Cape and Natal.
Although by no means the majority of those registered has been called up, their registration demonstrates how the war in South Africa is inextricably extending itself to all sections of white society.

Back on the border, almost all farmers within 50km of the border are now in the local Commandos. What is more with the establishment of an integrated Military Area Network (MARNET) of radio communications these farmers have become the eyes and ears of the SADF in suppressing the growing resistance to Apartheid. There is little doubt that as resistance to Apartheid has mounted in the rural areas, so the ANC has increased the internal training of its combatants in the rural areas. These combatants are then absorbed into the local population and further strengthen these communities in their resistance. The increasing use of landmines in rural areas (17 in 1986) is symptomatic of the growing support the ANC has in the rural areas and the increasing success it is having in recruiting combatants locally. Given the strategic significance of the obligations laid on rural whites by the government through the the Commando structures and the MARNET system, it seems likely that just as in the townships government informers and Council Police have become a target of popular resistance, so white farmers will also become a target, for they are increasingly indistinguishable from the SAP and SADF in the functions they perform in rural areas.
Thus the embroilment of the whole white rural population in the defence of Apartheid is generating a civil war situation (in the sense that the

(41) ibid. (42) Resister No. 42, February/March 1986.

civilian population on both sides is being increasingly embroiled in the daily conflict) which bodes ill for the future as the line between civilian and military personnel disappears. This is a serious development, for as the Commonwealth Eminent Persons Group warned, escalation of violence is sowing the seeds of the worst holocaust since the Second World War.

A CITIZEN FORCE CONSCRIPT DESCRIBES HIS EXPERIENCE OF DEPLOYMENT IN THE RURAL AREAS

"The whole thing started as a brown envelope for a call up in the Christmas holidays. It was for two months from 6 December 1985 to 6 February 1986 with the Natalia regiment... The first exercise was on the border of Natal and Swaziland where we began to monitor and capture people moving into Swaziland. It was a fruitless task because most of those detained and interrogated detailed the advantages of shopping in Swaziland and then returning to South Africa.

As SADF members and in our mode of operations we could not identify the enemy. That was the central weakness. When we were on patrol and entered a kraal you could sense the presence of the ANC and that the people were 100% behind them. In the end it became frustrating asking for information about guerrilla activities because you knew deep down that if you were in their position then you would also harbour and assist MK (Umkhonto we Sizwe)... Two exercises remain embedded in my memory, however.

The first was an operation to capture a man believed to be responsible for co-ordinating ANC activities in the area. At midnight we had moved into position approximately four kilometres from the kraal with other units on the other side. At 04.00 we moved in on the kraal and reached there at sunrise. We were expectantly sensing a successful capture. But we were confronted by the women and children, with no men in sight."

Resister

3.4 The War in the Townships

Since the Soweto uprising in 1976 the struggle in the black townships of South Africa has increasingly been seen as the focal point of the liberation struggle. During the 1976-77 revolts the SADF was mobilised and placed on stand-by but on the whole was mainly used in a back-up role in support of the police.

In April 1978 the SADF was used in a cordon operation in the Vaal for the first time. Since then the SADF has been repeatedly used in the townships, particularly in 1980-81 when they were mobilised in response to strikes and student unrest and since September 1984 there has been a permanent military presence in the townships. This greater use of the SADF against the black population of South Africa prompted the government to amend the Defence Act in June 1981 specifically to allow SADF units to be mobilised for "the suppression of internal disorder". By January 1983, according to official government sources, an average of 2,400 SADF troops were being used in police operations every month[43].

As the South African government moved towards its grand Apartheid goals, through both a restructuring of black local authorities and influx control, and through the proposed Tricameral Parliament, designed to bring the Indian and Coloured Communities into a junior partnership role in government, so popular resistance escalated. In January 1983 a steering committee was established to bring all progressive forces into a United Democratic Front in opposition to the government's constitutional proposals, which were seen by the black majority as a means of entrenching Apartheid. On 20 August 1983 the UDF was officially launched by 1,000 delegates representing 575 organisations. The government responded with an immediate campaign of harassment: banning meetings and rallies detaining many UDF supporters and harassing others. As the government's campaign of repression intensified in an attempt to stifle all opposition to its constitutional proposals, so confrontations between township residents and the police escalated. As a result throughout 1983-84 the SADF was more and more regularly deployed alongside the police in an intimidatory show of force.

Soon tens of thousands of troops were involved in the townships, mostly mobilised Citizen Force members who had already completed their two years of national service. Initially the government attempted to keep the SADF and the SAP roles distinct, in order to avoid sullying the image of the SADF through its association with police atrocities. However, as more and more troops were deployed the roles of the SADF and the SAP became indistinguishable. Often joint SADF/SAP patrols would be mounted with SADF and SAP personnel being deployed in the same Casspirs, and SADF personnel like the police were soon involved in rapes, robberies, unprovoked assaults and brutal torture.

In 1985, according to Defence Minister Malan's own admission, some 35,372 troops were deployed in the townships. This was more than the entire call up for 1985, in which the 'new' South African citizens affected by the 1984 Citizenship Amendment Act were targeted for conscription. This means that a high percentage of national servicemen deployed in the townships probably also enjoyed

(43) cited in Resister No. 37.

European citizenship. The troops deployed in the townships represented fully 33% of the strength of South Africa's regular army force[44] (this includes 64,000 national servicemen, 18,000 Permanent Force soldiers and the pool of manpower available from the Citizen Force at any one time – but excludes the 21,000 strong SWATF). These troops were in addition to units of the South Africa Police. This high level of mobilisation for repression in the townships has been sustained for over three years.

The military significance of the additional 46,000 citizens made eligible for conscription under the 1984 Citizenship Amendment Act can thus be appreciated. So too can the importance of bringing an extra 800,000 men, a large number of whom enjoy European citizenship or potential rights to European citizenship, into the Commando system, where they are increasingly helping to carry the burden of administrative duties and static defensive roles (it will be recalled that in 1983 Defence Minister Malan estimated that 7 support personnel were required for every serviceman deployed on active duty). Not only are European citizens actively participating in the bloody suppression of resistance in the townships, the images of which have horrified European public opinion, but they are also making a major contribution to the slaughter in the townships through the non-combat support roles they play in the SADF. The significance of this passive military role in repression was eloquently denounced by Dr Ivan Toms, the first officer to refuse to serve in the SADF, who argued that accepting non-combatant status aided Apartheid "just as much as those people who pull the trigger".

If a young European national is deployed by the SADF in the townships what is he likely to be called upon to do?

At a routine level most of his time whilst deployed in the townships would be spent patrolling the townships in an armoured vehicle. Initially it may be a bit of a joyride with an atmosphere of keen anticipation prevailing. Soon however, particularly if the troops are deployed jointly with SAP personnel, the anticipation will give way to frenzied excitement as police provocation brings a response of defiance from township residents and a burst of activity involving beating and whipping of township residents. It will probably involve the use of teargas, rubber bullets and even live ammunition against groups of people who congregate on street corners or outside houses. Regularly it results in the deaths of young black South Africans.

The SADF may also be involved in joint house-to-house searches with the police. For this purpose legislation was passed to extend

(44) IISS The Military Balance 1986-87 put South Africa's regular armed forces at 106,400 personnel.

police powers to any member of the Security Forces.

THE CASE OF DR. IVAN TOMS Dr. Ivan Toms, 35 risks detention, court martial and nearly three years in military detention barracks after he refuses to serve in the SADF. He is one of a growing number of white male South Africans publicly refusing to serve in the army now that the boundaries of war have contracted to the townships.

"There is a 95% chance that I'll end up in jail", he said during a countrywide tour to call for constructive alternatives to conscription.

"I can't go from treating injuries at my township clinic to putting on a uniform and causing those injuries."

His view was that non-combattant status aided Apartheid "just as much as those people who pull the trigger."

Dr. Toms is the first officer to refuse to serve in the army, after being the only doctor to serve the 130,000 squatters at Crossroads outside Cape Town. Dr. Toms is now serving a 634 days prison sentence for his stand against Apartheid.

"A sudden hail of stones is just what they've been waiting for. "Yahoo, let's go! and we launch into a hurtling, lurching circuit, past streams of panicking, running people, pumping gas and rubber bullets. It's all over in a couple of minutes: the cops have reached for their shot guns for the second round but the crowd has dispersed. The whole thing had the atmosphere of sport: kaffir baiting, beating and hunting".
Statement by National Serviceman

"Another night, another fire, we are hanging around while the fire tanker does its work when individual stones start dropping about us with deceiving harmlessness. Suddenly one smashes the windscreen of an SAP bakkie and two cops with shotguns bound off like dogs off a leash. They stalk the loe stone thrower and corner him; he continues his desperate barrage. They shoot him dead. He is about sixteen. He is a kill."
Statement by National Serviceman

"The presence of the army in the townships is a situation of conflict and war. No normal community life can reign with the army in our midst. Soweto is regarded as an area under siege by the army. The army is a serious source of conflict in Soweto. The army generally over-reacts and thus aggrevates an already sensitive situation. Many young people were shot dead at the lightest provocation. The army reminds young people that they are oppressed at gun point... the intervention of the army in the schools has disrupted the normal

45

Initially the SADF personnel were merely used to form the cordon in
these house-to-house searches but increasingly they have been
deployed in the actual process of searching itself.

With the imposition of the State of Emergency all Security Forces
personnel were granted indemnity from prosecution and this has led to
operations being conducted with extreme brutality, with cases of
indiscriminate assault, rape and torture having all been documented by
church leaders.

The young people of South Africa have since 1976 played a leading role
in opposition to Apartheid and school boycotts have been a principal
feature of the intensified resistance in the 1980s. This has led to the
South African Security Forces waging a particularly brutal war against
black school children. The SADF and SAP have on a number of
occasions attacked schools carrying out mass arrests. This has
resulted in over 2,500 children being held in detention in South Africa.
The army and police have also been used to force children back to
school in an attempt to break the schools boycott, with some schools
even being occupied by the SADF to ensure children stay in class.

Breaking all forms of resistance is the principal focus of SADF activities
in the townships. They have been used not only to break school
boycotts but also consumer boycotts, which are a major form of non-
violent resistance. Troops have even been used to break strikes. At the
Baragwanath Hospital in Soweto striking nurses and auxiliary staff
were rounded up by troops at gun-point and forced to accept their
dismissal pay, following a prolonged strike. In addition to strike-
breaking at hospitals, troops have been sent scouring black hospitals in
search of persons with injuries sustained during police and army
operations. Upon discovery these patients are forcibly removed and
placed in detention, on the assumption that since they are injured they
must have been involved in attacking the Security Forces!

A number of townships are now surrounded by razor wire fencing with
access into and out of the townships controlled by police roadblocks.
These sustained 24-hour-a-day operations against the townships have

required the establishment of army bases alongside the townships. Such a high profile troop presence in the townships has brought about widespread international condemnation and it is in response to this that the South African government has tried to reduce the need for SADF personnel. A first step in this process was to redeploy 6,000 para-military police from border duties into the townships. The South African Railways Police was then absorbed into the regular police in October 1986 and a further 15,000 Municipal Police and Special Constables (largely drawn from vigilante groups) recruited. By 1987 the Police Force strength including reserves had risen to 92,000. Of the 56,000 full-time police some 80% had been deployed in countering popular resistance to Apartheid in 1986. The long term aim is thus to reduce the visible deployment of troops in the townships, for not only is their deployment leading to further international condemnation but it is also bringing home to many white South Africans the reality of the civil war which is taking place in South Africa. However, there is little likelihood of troops being withdrawn from township operations – the Minister of Defence now refuses to disclose how many troops are involved, but in many areas they are a permanent feature.

THE POLICIES OF EUROPEAN GOVERNMENTS TOWARDS SOUTHERN AFRICA

All governments of the Community both individually and collectively have condemned Apartheid and South Africa's illegal occupation of Namibia. All are bound to the nine independent states of Southern Africa by an extensive trade and cooperation agreement known as the Lomé Convention. This Convention in an annex explicitly proclaims the determination of the contracting parties to:

"work effectively for the eradication of Apartheid which constitutes a violation of human rights and an affront to human dignity."[45]

Member states' bilateral policies towards independent Southern Africa are similar at a rhetorical level. But in the face of South Africa's military aggression against the region they have shown marked differences in the level of material and political support extended to the region.

.1 The Case of Italy, France and Greece

One of the major features of independent Southern Africa's relations with the EC over the past seven years has been the expanding involvement of Italy and France in the economic development efforts of the region. Prior to the formation of the Southern African Development Co-ordination Conference (SADCC) in April 1980, their involvement in the SADCC region was insignificant. However, by 1985 Italian net disbursements of overseas development assistance to the SADCC states accounted for 16.6% of the total amount received from EC member states, whilst France accounted for 6.3%. Italian and French support has been particularly focussed on the SADCC's Programme of Action which is designed to reduce the region's economic dependence on South Africa. All in all, since the formation of the SADCC Italy has contributed US$ 150 million to the SADCC Programme of Action and France over US$43 million. This development cooperation has resulted in the region increasing in importance as a market for French and Italian exports, despite the fact that South Africa's war against the region has cost over US$25 billion in lost income and devastated infrastructure since 1980.

"Italians that stayed became a respected community in South Africa. I would like to say on behalf of the South African government, that we are proud of you."
P.W. Botha, President of South Africa, 3rd November 1985.

(45) Lome Convention, Annex I, Joint Declaration on Article 4.

Both France and Italy have recognised, in the light of this brutal reality, the damaging consequences for the region which the perpetuation of Apartheid in South Africa entails. Since 1984 the Italian government has been providing substantial logistical support to enable the Mozambican army to protect Italian-financed development projects from MNR attack. It was furthermore under the Italian Presidency of the European Community that the question was first raised of the possible extension of non-lethal military assistance to Mozambique from Community resources. Initially this met with some resistance from other member states, but in November 1987 the Commission of the European Community (CEC) agreed a package of non-lethal military aid for troops guarding various CEC development projects in Mozambique. Indications are that just over £ 5 million will be available from Community resources under the Lome Convention for the provision of non-lethal military assistance to defend Community-financed development projects.

In the past year three French military evaluation missions have visited Mozambique with the aim of assessing the equipment needs for the protection of the Nacala railway line, the rehabilitation of which has been strongly supported by the French government. This Italian, French and Community military assistance, welcome as it is, contrasts markedly with the manner in which the French and Italian governments ignore completely the participation of that portion of the between 1.4 million and 2.1 million EC citizens (or potential community citizens)[46] resident in South Africa who are eligible for conscription into the various structures of the SADF. This includes some of the 8,000 French and 50,000 Italian citizens resident in South Africa. French and Italian citizens are participating in the SADF and fighting in defence of Apartheid, despite the fact that the legal basis exists in both France and Italy for the French and Italian governments to take immediate action to prohibit their citizens from entering South African military service, on pain of loss of citizenship.

Given both the French and Italian governments' stated policy of support for the SADCC and the recognised need for military assistance in defending SADCC states from South African aggression, does not the participation of their nationals in the SADF suggest an inconsistency in government policy?

If French and Italian policy is to be consistent and credible in Southern Africa, is not some action required to halt the participation of their citizens in the armed defence of Apartheid?

The Greek government in turn has spoken at SADCC meetings of its determination

"to deepen and enlarge its economic and technical cooperation with the member states of the SADCC."[47]

---

(46) See Inset on p. 48.
(47) SADCC Maseru (SADCC 1983), p.285.

The Greek government has, however, also spoken of the numerous Greek communities which exist almost everywhere in the world *"constituting important economic and social elements for their country of adoption."* [48]

This is indeed the case in South Africa. In October 1982 before the Federation of Hellenic Communities of South Africa P.W. Botha appealed to Greeks to accept South African citizenship[49].
There are currently some 80,000 Greek citizens living in South Africa, 40,000 of whom also hold South African citizenship[50]. Since 1982 these Greeks will have increasingly been embroiled in the defence of Apartheid. Yet the Greek government in line with its stated determination to deepen links with the SADCC region could prevent Greek citizens from participating in defence of Apartheid. Under Greek law, citizenship may be forfeited if a citizen undertakes acts incompatible with Greek status and in violation of Greek interests. A statement by the Greek government to the effect that service in the SADF was a violation of Greek interests would force Greeks resident in South Africa to choose between fighting in defence of Apartheid and losing their Greek nationality. This would pose a serious dilemma for Greeks resident in South Africa and could add to the manpower constraints faced by the repressive apparatus of the South African state.

4.2 Portugal, The United Kingdom, Germany and Belgium

Both Portugal and the UK have a long-standing involvement in Southern Africa. For Portugal the presence of some 600,000 Portuguese citizens in South Africa is a major source of concern. If a situation were ever to arise in which these citizens were to return to Portugal then the economic and social dislocation to Portuguese society would be dramatic. This has tended to be an over-riding factor in Portugal's policy towards the Southern African region.

The United Kingdom for its part is a major financial and trading partner of South Africa, with South Africa itself being the UK's largest export market outside of Europe and North America. There are furthermore, according to Malcolm Rifkind, who was the Foreign Office Minister responsible for Southern African affairs at the time, up to I million people now living in South Africa who would be entitled to settle in Britain if they so choose.[51]

The Federal Republic of Germany is also a major trading and investment partner of South Africa with some I00,000 of its citizens resident in South Africa.

(48) ibid. (49) Star, 19.10.82. (50) Letter Greek Embassy Netherlands to the AABN, 6.10.87.
(51) Business Day, 25.10.85.

51

All in all, over 35% of the white South African population have a citizenship link with one of these three countries (i.e. are either citizens or hold rights to citizenship) whilst at least 82% of this group also hold South African citizenship. Eight out of ten adult males in this group are thereby liable for conscription into the SADF. All in all citizens (or potential citizens) of these three countries alone constitute up to 30% of the SADF strength.[52] *See note 52 on page 55*

The German government has repeatedly expressed its commitment to peaceful political solutions in Southern Africa and has in detail condemned the Apartheid system. In Gaborone in February 1987 the German delegate to SADCC's Consultative Conference spoke of the mounting tension in Southern Africa and the disappointing performance of the South African government in introducing reforms, concluding that:

"there is nonetheless no alternative to continued efforts to bring about a reduction of external and internal use of violence in its various manifestations and, finally, peace."[53]

These "continued efforts" however were not held to extend to the prevention of German nationals participating in Apartheid's war throughout the region. Indeed there is no provision in German law for the loss of German citizenship arising from service in the armed forces of a foreign power. This is likewise the case in Portugal and the United Kingdom. The Portuguese government does not shirk from condemnation of the Apartheid regime and the territorial violations perpetrated by its armed forces. Yet serving Portuguese army officers have on occasion visited the bases of South Africa's principal instrument of aggression, the MNR, inside Mozambique, thereby extending a form of recognition to the perpetrators of some of the most horrendous crimes recorded this decade[54]. Despite the fact that the Portuguese government is considering extending military assistance to Mozambique, its commitment to fostering peaceful solutions and reconciliation in Southern Africa is not held to extend to the activities of its own nationals in South Africa, many of whom with support from residents in Portugal itself, have made themselves the principal agents of destabilisation in the region.

The British government has proved itself the most forthright conservative government in its response to the involvement of European citizens in the armed defence of Apartheid. Prior to the September 1985 EC decision to harmonise policy in the sphere of military cooperation, the British government had already announced that the extension of South African Citizenship involved in the 1984 South African Citizenship Amendment Act did not at that time affect a

(53) SADCC Gaborone (SADCC 1987), p.112.
(54) See J. Hanlon, Beggar Your Neighbours (CIIR 1986), p.147.

British citizen's status and that furthermore no measure was to be drawn up to withdraw British nationality from British citizens serving in the South African army or police.[55] This announcement was made despite the fact that British citizens had been involved in some of the most notorious acts of aggression and destabilisation committed by the SADF against the independent states of Southern Africa. It was, however, fully consistent with a government statement made in 1983 by the then British Defence Minister Michael Heseltine, following revelations concerning the involvement of Lt. Alan Gingles in sabotaging the Beira railway line in Mozambique in 1981, to the effect that the British government would not stop former British Army personnel from joining the SADF.

In the light of this acquiescence in its citizens' involvement in destabilisation, announcement of the British government's decision to help train Mozambican and Zimbabwean officers leads one to question the coherence of its approach to military issues in Southern Africa.

The view that no measures should be taken against European citizens serving in the SADF appears to be widely accepted by other governments in Europe, in part because it is fully consistent with existing practice. In the case of Belgium, for example, dual nationality citizens (approximately 25,000 people) resident in South Africa are free to choose in which armed forces they wish to carry out their national service. Indeed, in response to a letter on this issue to the Permanent Representatives of EC Member States to the Community, the British and Dutch ambassadors were kind enough to indicate that the League of Nations Protocol relating to Military Obligations in Certain Cases of Double Nationality (The Hague, April 12, 1930) applied. This protocol was signed by all member states with the exception of Italy, Ireland and Denmark. According to our present information this protocol has been ratified only by the UK, Belgium and the Netherlands – and South Africa. In the case of the UK since the ending of conscription the provisions no longer apply. However according to the South African army magazine Paratus (August 1984, Supplement) a number of countries who have not ratified the protocol nevertheless apply its provisions (or similar provisions) to South Africans holding dual nationality.

BELGIANS IN SOUTH AFRICA

Well before the 1982 and 1984 legislation Belgians have been involved in South Africa's military programme. One Belgian citizen from Mechelen when interviewed admitted that he served in South Africa's 'Dad's Army'' (the Commandos). In 1968 he emigrated to South Africa to "escape my military

(55) Sunday Express, 17.4.83.

service". He married a South African and has dual citizenship. "I feel completely at home here. I'm a South African citizen but I also still have Belgian nationality." Any reference to discrimination in "his country" rather upset this Belgian citizen. In the 20 years he has lived amongst Afrikaners he has adopted their racism and reasoning. He is convinced of the racial inferiority of blacks ("has Africa ever produced an Einstein"). He justifies Apartheid or separate development as the only answer to the country's problems. According to him whites arrived first in South Africa (1968?) and they conquered large parts of the country in an honest way from the blacks.

Que. "Is the crisis deepening in South Africa?"

Ans. "Maybe yes, but we are prepared."

Que. "Do you belong to the Dad's Army?"

Ans. "Yes, I can see you are well informed."

Que. "If your unit calls you up to patrol in the streets of Soweto, would you then shoot black children if you were ordered to?"

Ans. "Sure. Why not?"

Que. "You say Nelson Mandela is a terrorist leader. Do you know him, have you ever read books by him?"

Ans. "Sure I know him and I did read some of his writings."

Que. "So you've had banned books in your possession?"

Ans. "Well, no, I didn't really read them but we all know anyway that Nelson Mandela wants to overthrow the whites through terror."

Apartheid: De Rotte Appel p. 11, Socialistische Solidariteit

According to Paratus:

"In terms of an agreement between the RSA and several other countries a person possessing two or more nationalities who habitually resides in one of the countries whose nationality he possesses, and who is in fact most closely connected with that country shall be exempt from all military obligations in the other country or countries." [56]

The countries listed as being party to this agreement include: Great Britain, Germany, France, Greece, Portugal, Belgium, Holland, Spain and Luxembourg. This official governmental acquiesence in at least Belgium and the Netherlands stands in stark contrast to statements condemning violence and in favour of peaceful change in South Africa.

4.3 The Netherlands, Ireland and Denmark

The Dutch and Danish governments have long been in the forefront of the European campaign to secure Namibian independence, eliminate Apartheid and support the efforts of the SADCC. It was only to be expected therefore, that the Dutch government should be in the

(56) Paratus Supplement, August 1984.

forefront of reducing military cooperation with South Africa. On 20 October 1982 the Dutch government, in response to Parliamentary questioning announced that no permission will be granted for voluntary service in the South African armed forces, and that disregard of this rule would result automatically in the deprivation of Dutch nationality.

However, it was also pointed out that the fulfilment of compulsory military service in a foreign army does not result in the deprivation of Dutch nationality when a new Dutch Citizenship law came into force. Immediately following the South African Citizenship Amendment Act the Dutch Consul General in South Africa S. Siedenburg announced that Dutch citizens would not lose their citizenship as a result of the Act[57]. The legal position in this regard was regularised in January 1985. There are currently around 40,000 Dutch citizens resident in South Africa, with perhaps a further 160,000 being eligible for Dutch citizenship (see note B p. 56).

Not only do these 200.000 eligible Dutch in South Africa not endanger their Dutch citizenship or their right thereof when they serve in the SADF, but they are freed by this job from their Dutch national service obligations if they should return to Holland.
This contrasts strongly with the official Dutch policy and casts doubt on the intensity of the Dutch government anti-Apartheid protestations.

Since an insignificant number of Danes reside in South Africa, the question of the participation of European citizens in the SADF has not yet become an issue in Denmark. However, this does not mean that the Danish government should not be concerned about this issue, for under EC regulations leading to the completion of the internal market in 1992, Denmark too will have to extend all the rights of abode and work seeking to the between 1.3 million and 2.1 million EC citizens in South Africa who may one day return to Europe, having played their part in the destruction and devastation of their adopted country, South Africa.

This common European citizenship to which the Community is moving means that the question of British, German, Portuguese, Italian, Dutch, Belgian, French, Greek and Irish citizens in South Africa is not simply a source of concern to their respective governments, but impinges upon all member states of the European Community and as such needs to be considered by the European Community as a whole.
Before 31.12.92 a solution needs to be found for the right of return for citizens or eligible citizens of member states of the European Community, and especially for those coming from South Africa and having served in the SADF.
In the case of Ireland, it was estimated that between 20,000 and 25,000 South African citizens may claim Irish citizenship, though this could be

(57) See Rand Daily Mail, 12.10.84.

up to three times larger, reaching a total of up to 75,000[58]. In 1985-86 alone 2,400 South African citizens applied for Irish citizenship, up from an insignificant number in the preceding years. This upsurge in South African applications for Irish citizenship was in part the result of pending changes in Irish citizenship laws and in part the result of the deepening crisis in South Africa.

Ethnic Irish South Africans would feel quite at home in the SADF where the 22 Field Regiment is now known as the South African Irish Regiment. This regiment was one of the last regiments to withdraw from Angola in 1976 during the first South African invasion of Angola. Since then the South African Irish have been regularly deployed in Namibia. Although the regiment is now ethnically diverse, the association of Ireland with the brutal and illegal acts perpetrated by this regiment reflects poorly on Ireland.

At a European level, although a number of countries (France, Italy, Holland and Denmark) have been developing a growing positive involvement in the SADCC region and even the conservative British and West German governments are now recognising the need to reduce the SADCC region's dependence on South Africa, the continued involvement of European citizens in the SADF highlights the inconsistency of Europe's approach to the crisis in South Africa.

WHITES IN SOUTH AFRICA, HOLDING OR ENTITLED TO A EUROPEAN CITIZENSHIP

Country	Currently holding a European citizenship	Currently holding, eligible or undetermined
UK	500,000	1,000,000 (A)
Portugal	600,000	600,000
Germany	100,000	100,000
Italy	50,000	50,000
Holland	40,000	200,000 (B)
Belgium	25,000	25,000
France	8,000	8,000
Greece	80,000	80,000
Ireland	2,400	75,000 (C)
TOTAL	1,405,400	2,138,000 (D)

(A) Source: British Foreign Office via British embassy in The Hague. The discrepancy arises because many SA citizens are eligible for UK citizenship

(58) See Irish Times, 19.11.86.

and may at some time in the future chose to exercise this right. See comments by Malcolm Rifkind cited in Business Day 25.10.85.

(B) The discrepancy in the Dutch figures arise because many SA citizens are eligible for Dutch citizenship and may at some future date choose to exercise this right. The estimate of 200,000 is the Dutch government's own estimate.

(C) It is difficult to ascertain how many Irish passport holders are resident in SA. The figure of 2,400 applies only to recent applications from SA for Irish citizenship (1985-86). The figure of 75,000 represents an Irish Foreign Affairs maximum estimate of how many SA citizens may be eligible for Irish citizenship. See Irish Times 19.11.86.

(D) The figures for Germany, Italy, Belgium and France are taken from the Financial Mail (SA) 18.10.85. The estimates in the Financial Mail for the UK, Portugal and Holland were lower than the figures provided by the respective embassies and Ministries. Consequently, the figures quoted for the UK and Portugal are those provided by the embassies accredited to the Netherlands. The Greek figures are taken from a letter dated 6.10.87 from the Greek embassy to the Netherlands to the Dutch Anti-Apartheid Movement (AABN).

(52) The total white population of South Africa on December 31st 1984 was 4,845,000 (10% of which were non South African citizens), of which 600,000 have a citizenship link with Portugal, 1,000,000 with the UK and 100,000 with the Federal Republic of Germany. This combined total (1,700,000) represents 35% of the total white population of South Africa. Of this 35% 301,000 did not have South African citizenship (18% of the 1,700,000). The male population in the approximately 1,4 million South African citizens with a citizenship link with Portugal, the UK and Germany are eligible for conscription into the various arms of the SADF. Assuming an even age and sex distribution across the whole of the white South African population this implies that up to 32 % of the strength of the SADF could be drawn from whites with a citizenship link to one of these three countries. As immigrants tend to be young males, this would be an underestimate.

5 RESISTANCE AGAINST EXTENDED CONSCRIPTION AND THE EUROPEAN RESPONSE

5.1 The Position of the Church in South Africa.

The South African Churches have become deeply disturbed at the path of confrontation which the extension of conscription represented and both the Catholic and Protestant Church have now addressed themselves to the moral and ethical dimensions of fighting in defence of an unjust system, by throwing their full support behind the right to object to military service. It is the churches' belief, as expressed by the Southern African Catholic Bishops Conference (SACBC) and the South African Council of Churches (SACC), that the denial of basic human rights to the majority of South Africans and the unequal distribution of land and wealth is the root cause of violence in South Africa. If the escalating cycle of violence is to be broken then it is essential that the root cause of injustice and inequality be addressed, for only if this is done can a lasting peace be brought to South Africa. How, then, can a war fought in defence of such an heretical system of injustice and inequality be a just war?

As early as 1974 the South African Council of Churches had sought to place the issue of individual moral decision in the context of the justice of the cause for which the individual was being called up. This took the SACC beyond the universal pacifist position as the basis for rejecting military service, to the specific context of Apartheid in South Africa. The SACC position was supported by Catholic Archbishop Hurley who summed up his own position in four brief statements:

1. If South Africa gets involved in a border war, this war will have been provoked by the policy of Apartheid.
2. To defend white South African society by force of arms is to defend the policy of Apartheid.
3. To defend Apartheid is to defend an unjust cause.
4. It is not permissible for Christians to fight an unjust war.

This line of reasoning underpinned the stand of a number of early conscientious objectors in South Africa. The Churches' opposition to the militarisation of South African society has inevitably brought them into conflict with the South African state. As the situation has deteriorated with regard to South Africa's war against its neighbours, its war in Namibia and its war against its own people inside South Africa, so the churches have been forced to adopt stronger and stronger positions. Currently the Catholic church is considering an appeal to foreign governments to grant political asylum and refugee status to South African conscientious objectors. This action is based on the Catholic church's firm believe that the SADF and those serving in it are engaged in regular contraventions of international law by illegally occupying Namibia and by raids into neighbouring countries. The Catholic Church has furthermore highlighted how the SADF is used as a political weapon against community leaders and communities inside South Africa, through its occupation of black residential areas and through assisting the South African Police in detaining large numbers of people. The Church is now putting its full weight behind the growing opposition to conscription, as expressed both through the vehicle of the End Conscription Campaign and the Conscientious Objectors Support Groups. This move towards an implicit condemnation of the role of the SADF and an open call to the international community to support Conscientious Objectors, demonstrates fully the church's rejection of the militarisation of South African society and its grave concern about the implications for the whole of Southern Africa.

THE END CONSCRIPTION CAMPAIGN

In 1983, as the result of an initiative taken by the Black Sash, the End Conscription Campaign was formed.

Since its formation it has gained the support of over 50 organisations for its call to end conscription, including amongst others the South African Council of Churches (SACC) the United Democratic Front (UDF), Southern African Catholic Bishops Conference (SACBC), the National Union of South African Students (NUSAS) and the Johannesburg Democratic Action Committee (JODAC).

By 1985 it had branches in Cape Town, Durban, Grahamstown, Johannesburg, Pietermaritzburg and Port Elizabeth.

The ECC is constantly walking on eggs, for under the Defence Act it is an offence to call on people to refuse the call up, punishable by six months in prison or a R5,000 fine.

The State has become increasingly concerned about the impact of the ECC campaign and has moved against its activists, attempting to associate them with the ANC, presumably as a prelude to the banning of the organisation.

The ECC campaign has increasingly focussed white opinion on the war taking place in the townships and has, even if equivocably, gained support from sections of the liberal Progressive Federal Party (PFP) for its campaign.

This courageous resistance by young white South Africans demands the support of European governments, not their acquiescence in sowing the seeds of destruction in Southern Africa.

.2 Responses to Extended Conscription inside South Africa

How have European citizens in South Africa responded to their conscription into the South African armed forces? The first point to make is that European citizens were already participating in defence of Apartheid on a voluntary basis at all levels before both the 1982 and 1984 extensions of the call up. European professional soldiers were signed up for the Permanent Force in increasing numbers from the mid-1970s, whilst young European immigrants have been volunteering for national service since conscription was introduced in 1957. However especially since 1982 European citizens have been drawn into the defence of Apartheid on a larger scale as a matter of routine. It is this routine involvement in an increasingly violent conflict within South Africa which has led to the development of a serious challenge to the whole system of conscription.

The first response to the 1984 measure within the immigrant community was an increase in emigration by some 20%, whilst migration to South Africa dropped by 25%[59]. In the immediate aftermath of the April 1984 Citizenship Amendment Act a total of 1,335 immigrants signed declarations stating that they did not wish to become South African citizens. Of this 1,335 fully 84% were males, with the principal underlying cause being the concomitant obligations to serve in the SADF in defence of Apartheid.[60] In January 1985, 7,589 conscripts failed to answer their call up, compared with 1,596 in the whole of 1984.[61] In January 1986 the Minister of Defence refused to provide figures on the number of conscripts failing to answer their call up on the basis that "it is not in the public interest".[62]

Many of these young South Africans are either forced to live underground existences within South Africa or to flee the country. Some of them, however, prefer to make a stand, and on religious, moral and political grounds have refused to undertake military service in the SADF. These young men have received long prison sentences. Nevertheless resistance to service in the SADF has expanded remarkably over the past three years as troops have increasingly been deployed in the townships of South Africa.

Although the majority continue to render service in defence of white privilege, which the current government of South Africa is committed to

(59) Business Day, 4.9.1985. (60) Star, 13.4.85. (61) ibid. (62) cited in Resister No. 49.

perpetuating, a growing minority are actively opposing this unjust war. At an organisational level there is the End Conscription Campaign, which has through its campaigns breached the walls of media censorship which hides the horror of the war in the townships from white South Africans. As a result the ECC has come under intense pressure from the South African government.

On 3 August 1987 organisational and individual aspects of resistance to the militarisation of South African society came together when 23 young conscripts joined together to publicly refuse to serve in the SADF. They released a joint statement which expressed the belief that

"our country is best served if we refuse to fight in the SADF. The laws of this country make this a serious step to take. Yet we feel there comes a time when moral choices, no matter how difficult, cannot be avoided.'[63]

Their brave stand is symptomatic of a growing unease at the slide towards civil war which is taking place and deserves the full support of the European Community both at a political and material level, something they have yet to receive.

There are others, however, who judge such a direct challenge to be too dangerous a course of action and these simply fail to answer their call up and go underground inside South Africa. Sometimes this proves too difficult and they are forced to flee the country and seek refuge abroad.

5.3 The European Governmental Response to Extended Conscription

What has been the response of European governments to the conscription of their nationals into the SADF in defence of Apartheid? At the time the new legislation came into force British government representatives in South Africa showed themselves to be ignorant of the implications of the SACAA and showed little inclination to assist British citizens who wished to avoid conscription into the SADF.

Questioned in Parliament in June 1986 as to any representations the British government may have made to the South African government concerning the effect on British citizens of the 1984 legislation, Lynda Chalker replied that the legislation:

"did not affect, and could not have affected, a British citizen's status as such'[64]

and that as a result no representations had been made to the South African government on the issue. A similar attitude was manifested by other European governments.

(63) ECC Focus, September 1987.
(64) Written Reply to Michael Meadowcroft (Leeds West) no. W166, 30 June 1986.

Overall in Europe, the view was taken that the acquisition of South African nationality under the 1984 legislation was an involuntary act and therefore, no citizen of a member state who entered the armed forces of South Africa would suffer any adverse consequences as a result of his action (despite the fact that in the case of Italy, France and Greece entry into the South African armed forces could result in the loss of nationality if the Italian or French governments specifically ordered its citizens not to undertake military service or if, in the case of Greece, the government declared participation in the South African armed forces to be contrary to Greek national interests).

This position, coupled with reciprocal arrangements in Holland and Belgium concerning military service obligations of dual nationals, leads one to conclude that European governments have done little to discourage their citizens from participating in the military defence of Apartheid. Indeed, not only have conservative governments in Europe succeeded in blocking the introduction of broad and effective economic sanctions, as a means of exerting real pressure for fundamental change, but they are in reality conniving in their citizens' participation in defence of Apartheid.

Within the positive measures approach favoured by conservative European governments it has been suggested that the European Community could support both the anti-militarisation campaign and organisations working to increase awareness amongst the white population on the need for political change. However, under the Community's Special Programme for victims of Apartheid at least one project aimed specifically at educating whites for change was excluded on the grounds that it was too politically sensitive. It seems ironic that extending financial and political support to organisations opposed to militarisation and advocating peaceful political change should be deemed too politically sensitive whilst the daily participation of several hundred thousand European citizens in the armed defence of Apartheid is not even deemed to be a political issue worthy of governmental concern.

5.4 The European Governmental Response to War Resisters

As early as December 1978 the United Nations unanimously adopted a resolution calling upon its members to grant asylum or safe transit to persons compelled to leave their country of nationality solely because of a conscientious objection to assisting in the enforcement of Apartheid through service in the military or police force. The following case studies are illustrative of the ambiguous positions adopted by European governments towards South African War Resisters.

5.4.1 The Netherlands: The Case of Erik van Hoekelen

In January 1985, as a result of the provisions of the 1984 Citizenship Amendment Act, a Dutch citizen, Erik van Hoekelen was conscripted into the SADF. Initially Erik was hesitant to participate in the SADF but under peer group pressure he finally opted to join the army. Having witnessed the brutal and repressive nature of the SADF, he soon regretted his decision and within six months had gone Absent without Leave (AWOL). In August 1985 he decided to desert from the South African army. He was captured and brought before a military court on 9 December 1985, where he was sentenced to 90 days in detention barracks, suspended for the length of his national service. He was ordered to report back to his unit on the 14 December. Erik however, reported to the South African Ministry of Home Affairs, where he sought to cancel his South African citizenship. Initially the Ministry of Home Affairs refused to accept this application for cancellation, insisting that he first complete his national service. As a result van Hoekelen sought the assistance of the Dutch Consul. The attitude of the Dutch Consul, however, was nothing short of hostile and he rendered little or no assistance to Erik in his efforts to avoid fighting in defence of Apartheid. Instead he sought to reduce the issue to one of individual conscience and choice. After considerable legal argument Erik van Hoekelen was eventually permitted to leave South Africa for Holland. The case however, raised a number of disturbing questions concerning the Dutch government's attitude towards this aspect of military cooperation with South Africa. It seems that the Dutch government along with its European colleagues felt that the preparation of a brochure on the consequences of Apartheid was sufficient guidance for its citizens when faced with conscription into the SADF.

This brochure by the way, the government until now did not succeed in producing. The inadequacy of the response to those European citizens seeking to extricate themselves from military service in defence of Apartheid is matched only by the callousness of certain European governments to war resisters who seek refuge in Europe.

5.4.2 Germany: The Case of Hanno Rumpf

The German government has received no applications for political asylum from South African war resisters in large part because of the prohibitive nature of the interpretation laid on its asylum laws. However, the attitude of the West German government in its treatment of war resisters claiming German citizenship highlights the particular hostility which exists at a federal government level in Germany towards South African and Namibian war resisters. This is illustrated by the case of Hanno Rumpf.

Hanno Rumpf is a 30-year-old Namibian whose paternal grand-parents were German citizens and whose mother was a German citizen. In 1984 Hanno Rumpf, a SWAPO member, was forced to flee Namibia in order to avoid conscription into the South African army of occupation. Before leaving Namibia Hanno applied for West German citizenship on the basis that his father had had his West German citizenship restored. Hanno himself takes up the story:

"At the same time my two sisters and brother applied for citizenship of the FRG as well. About two or three months into 1985 they received their FRG citizenship. I did not receive my FRG citizenship at the time because I was told by the Department of the Interior in the FRG that my application was treated according to a different paragraph of the nationalisation laws in the FRG (due to the fact that my application was considered to have been filed within the FRG before I was naturalised.) I had to comply with certain demands stated in the law such as the fact that I had integrated myself into FRG society; and that I had to prove that I could make a living in the FRG. My attorney in Bremen where I lived ... told me that another demand of the re-naturalization law was that I would receive a security vetting by the relevant FRG authorities. At that stage I was quite active politically in West Germany for SWAPO, travelling most weekends to meetings to educate people with regard to the Namibian issue. At some stages I had the distinct impression that the same faces and people appeared at the meetings at which I spoke, and I concluded that this had something to do with the security vetting that I was supposed to receive before FRG citizenship was granted to me. The problem I had was that the actual granting of the citizenship dragged out for many months. At some stage I was close to receiving citizenship, and then my South African passport ran out, and on the very same day I was called by an official of the Federal Ministry of the Interior who told me that I should have my South African passport renewed immediately otherwise my permit of residence in the FRG would become invalid. I immediately contacted my lawyer and he told me that it seemed very clear to him that a legal basis from which they could deport me to South Africa was being created. It seemed that the government had taken a dislike to my policies and didn't want to make an FRG citizen out of me".

The political support extended to Hanno Rumpf by the Social Democratic controlled government in Bremen, prevented the Federal government from deporting him, but the Federal government did force Hanno Rumpf to renounce his South African citizenship. While he was willing, indeed keen to do this, it proved rather difficult, for the South African Consulate General in Hamburg declined to answer any of Hanno Rumpf's correspondence on this issue. It was only when Hanno Rumpf threatened to raise the matter both in the media and the Bundestag that

the difficulties were resolved and West German citizenship granted.
It seems strange that while Hanno Rumpf, a known opponent of
Apartheid and South Africa's illegal occupation of Namibia, should be
forced to give up his South African citizenship in order to gain West
German citizenship, thousands of German speaking Namibians and
South Africans are allowed to hold dual nationality, retaining their West
German citizenship despite their participation in South Africa's war
against the region and the continued illegal occupation of Namibia.

It appears as if the West German government has one set of rules for
those opposed to Apartheid and another for those who acquiesce in the
crimes of Apartheid. The West German government took no action
when one of its nationals, Gerald Eckert volunteered for the SADF in
July 1982, neither did it seek to withdraw German citizenship from Lt.
Eckert when in February 1983 he took out South African citizenship.
Their treatment of Gerald Eckert (who deserted from the SADF, fled to
Mozambique, returned to Germany and then returned once more to
South Africa) stands in marked contrast to their treatment of Hanno
Rumpf.

5.4.3 Belgium: The Case of Michael Healey

The callousness of European governments is further illustrated by the
case of Michael Healey, which came to light in Belgium in 1987. Michael
Healey was called up for service in the SADF in 1976. He became
known as a "nigger lover" because he refused to accept the racist
indoctrination of the SADF and after a few months he deserted. He
eluded capture for several months but was eventually captured and
court-martialled. He was sentenced to three months in detention
barracks after which time in August 1977 he was returned to his unit.
After only a few months he deserted once again, but this time
succeeded in eluding the authorities. He even managed to get a job and
whilst living a semi-clandestine existence met a Flemish girl who was
visiting South Africa. Their relationship developed and in October 1982
he accompanied her to Belgium on a visitor's visa. It was here that
Michael Healey made a major mistake. Relaxing after his ordeal of a life
on the run in South Africa he neglected to apply immediately for refugee
status. This did not become a problem until his relationship with his
girlfriend turned sour and their marriage plans were abandoned. He then
became acutely aware that he had no legal basis for his continued
residence in Belgium. Healey after considerable uncertainty and only
after receiving advice from COSAWR in Holland applied for refugee
status in Belgium. His request was turned down, because of the prior
irregularities in his residence, as was his subsequent appeal. Healey is
now in hiding from the Belgium authorities, in the full knowledge that
should he be apprehended he will be deported back to South Africa,

where he will face up to ten years in prison for desertion. After this he will be forced once again to return to his unit to complete his term of national service in the defence of Apartheid.

Although the case of Michael Healey is in some respects exceptional, his confusion and sense of security upon arriving in Europe is not all that uncommon, given the pressures placed on white South African youth. Although there are hundreds of South African war resisters who have been given refuge in Europe the treatment of Healey is symptomatic of the indifference shown by European governments to those whites, many of whom are also citizens of European countries, who are opposed to serving in defence of Apartheid. South African war resisters have to apply for refugee status and thereby take up part of the national allocation for refugees. These principled and courageous young men are partially ostracised for their opposition to fighting in defence of Apartheid, whilst mercenaries, volunteers and ordinary conscripts resident in South Africa who enjoy a European citizenship are free to enter Europe and live a normal life after committing untold crimes in defence of Apartheid.

4.4 Britain: A Reserved Attitude

In Britain government spokespersons have made it clear that all applications for asylum from South African war resisters are carefully considered on individual merit in accordance with the 1951 Convention relating to the status of refugees, and that an unwillingness to perform military service is not generally regarded in itself as sufficient grounds to justify the granting of rights of asylum and refugee status. However where opposition to military service is held to be based on other deeply held moral, religious or political beliefs which would result in the national authorities treating the applicant for refugee status more harshly than that normally accorded to those refusing military service, then the British government's position is that granting asylum might be appropriate. Where asylum is not granted the British government is willing to consider the granting of "exceptional leave to remain" in the UK.

Overall the British government's position seeks to give the government leeway in its handling of individual cases. This uncertainty seems designed to generate insecurity so that the asylum seeker feels constrained in the activities he may pursue in opposition to Apartheid whilst resident in the UK.

In view of UN resolutions on this issue and recent calls from the Church inside South Africa, what is required of the British government and other European governments is a clear declaration welcoming South African war resisters as an integral part of the European Community's stated anti-Apartheid stance.

PEACE NOW SADF OUT

End Conscription Campaign

ECC

End Conscription Campaign

CONCLUSIONS

Not only is the Community the largest investor in South Africa and its major trading partner, but apparently one third of South Africa's whites either hold EC passports or have a right to acquire one.

Because of the recent extensions of military service in South Africa in 1982 and 1984, EC/South African dual nationals now constitute one third of the South African armed forces. To white men in South Africa, military service means active involvement in the defence of Apartheid from the age of 18 to 55. The EC member countries choose to disregard their subjects' military activities in South Africa. There is only one exception. In the case of remigration (partial) fulfilment of military service in South Africa engenders exemption in some EC countries.

No EC country feels responsible for what its subjects do in South Africa. This keeps creating schizophrenic situations, for instance in the case of South Africa's terrorist activities in the frontline countries. They are condemned by the Community, but at the same time there is a proven involvement of EC subjects in these activities; non-lethal military aid is extended by EC member states to the countries of the SADCC to defend development projects threatened by South African Reconaissance Commando saboteurs or regular army units, whilst EC citizens commonly participate in these acts of state terrorism.

This brochure lays out how South Africa is able to keep up its war on three fronts (at home against the black population, in Namibia and against the Front-Line States) by including new groups of whites in compulsory military service and extending the duration of military service obligations. In the last two instances when the group eligible for military service was enlarged (in 1982 and 1984) it concerned large numbers of EC citizens. It is exactly this incorporation of Europeans which makes possible the continuation of this war on three fronts.

The incorporation of Europeans strengthens the military clout of the Apartheid regime and delays the moment when political solutions will have to be found. Therefore the "none of our business" approach of the EC to the extension of conscription to European citizens living in South Africa undermines the credibility of Europe's policy towards South Africa. The EC member states are on record as favouring a political solution, but when their citizens are used to try and enforce a military solution they sit by and do nothing.

EC countries have a strong interest in a political solution to the conflict in South Africa since over 2 million white South Africans are entitled to an EC passport. In view of EC moves towards the single internal market for employees and self-employed this should alarm not only Portugal and the UK but all EC countries.

Not all dual nationals with a right to an EC passport will contemplate repatriation to Europe in the case of a further escalation of confrontation in South Africa. Nevertheless, an EC passport is certainly considered a valuable insurance policy. Thus the EC has substantial possibilities to influence these dual nationals. Since one third of the white population is involved, it provides the EC with a powerful bargaining position towards South Africa. Any pressure brought to bear on even apart of this segment of the white population to prevent them fulfilling their military service can weaken the regime's military clout and jeopardise its struggle on any of the three fronts on which it wages its war.

Discouraging enlistment in the South African armed forces could be one of the most effective methods of depriving the Apartheid regime of its military options. The EC has excellent leverage to pursue a policy of discouraging the pursuit of a military solution, as one third of the current and future conscripts are EC subjects.

The militarisation of South African society has reached a point where neither inhabitants nor companies can remain neutral and prevent themselves from becoming part of the machinery which serves to perpetuate Apartheid. EC countries should face this reality and give up their myopia with regard to the complicity of their subjects and companies in the armed defence of Apartheid. If we condemn Apartheid, internal repression, the illegal occupation of Namibia and southern Angola and the destabilisation of the Front-Line States, then we must acknowledge that all this would not be possible without the active participation of EC citizens and the financial and logistical support provided by European companies. The credibility of the EC will depend on the measures it will take to put an end to this crucial role played by its subjects: on the one hand by making enlistment in the South African armed forces incompatible with the retention of an EC citizenship; on the other hand by banning European companies from making voluntary supplementary payments to South African conscripts and by demanding disinvestment should these supplementary payments become compulsory.

Positive measures may include a magnanimous policy on taking in South African draft dodgers. At present there is no such thing. Unfortunately, however, negative measures are essential as well. Depending on the legal possibilities in the respective EC countries, the return of EC citizens who have fulfilled their military service in South Africa must be made either more difficult or impossible. Obviously this means first of all that EC countries should no longer exempt anyone from military service because of fulfilment of this obligation in South Africa. In those countries which have this legal possibility already (France, Italy, Greece), fulfilment in South Africa should result in loss of European citizenship: the necessary legal measures should be taken. The posibilities to return to the European Community should be limited or completely ended for those binationals living in South Africa and Namibia and having served in the SADF or SWATF.

The as yet unaddressed problem of the right to return for people living outside the community and eligible for a citizenship of an EC member state should in this light be urgently addressed in the framework of the completion of the internal market.

Finally, the EC should prohibit companies with South African branches from making voluntary supplementary payments to their employees who fulfill their military service.

The publishers wish to thank a.o. OXFAM
Belgium and the National Committee on
Development Education (NCO) of the
Netherlands for their financial contribution.

Design by **Tineke Stevens**, Amsterdam
Typeset by **Janny Oei**, Amsterdam
Printed in Belgium by **Fotek**, St. Niklaas
Introduction and conclusions translated
by **Paul Kuiper**